DINOSAURS
THROUGH TIME

Amazing Dinosaurs was created and produced by
McRae Books Srl
Publishers: Anne McRae, Marco Nardi
Project Manager: Anne McRae
Graphic Design: Marco Nardi
Illustrations: Studio Stalio
Editing: Joanne Bertrand
Picture Research: Elzbieta Gontarska, Daniela Morini
Cutouts: Filippo Delle Monache, Alman Graphic Design
Layouts: Laura Ottina, Sebastiano Ranchetti

ISBN-10: 88-6098-042-9
ISBN-13: 978-88-6098-042-7

Color separations: Litocolor (Florence)
Printed and bound in Singapore

Rupert Matthews

DINOSAURS
THROUGH TIME

McRae Books

Contents

Henodus, page 17

Ammonite shell,
page 12

Coelophysis,
page 25

The Triassic world, page 8

*Peteinosaurus,
page 28*

Skull of an Eoraptor, page 8

Introduction

This book provides an overview of the age of dinosaurs, beginning with the devastating mass extinction at the end of the Permian Age that almost wiped out life on our planet. This was followed by the Triassic Period, which saw the rise of reptiles and the first dinosaurs, and then the Jurassic and Cretaceous Periods, when dinosaurs and their cousins in the seas and skies truly ruled the world. Dinosaurs became extinct about 65 million years ago, and the final section of this book examines the various theories that explain why they disappeared.

Coelophysis skeleton, page 8

How this book works

Each section in this book begins with a dynamic two-page illustrated scene that shows dinosaurs and other reptiles as they hunt, eat, and go about their daily lives. These are followed by double-page spreads with more text and illustrations that explain the concept introduced in the scene in greater detail.

Brief captions explain how each spot illustration relates to the subject.

Vivid, descriptive text accompanies the large illustration that introduces each four-page section.

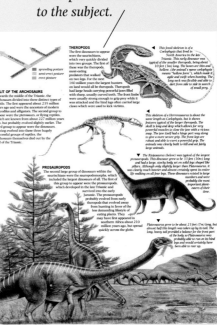

A dynamic, full-color illustration at the beginning of each section.

General text introduces the subject matter for each section.

Detailed illustrations highlight specific points.

CONTINENTAL DRIFT

The earth's crust is not one single sheet of solid material. It is divided into many vast rafts of rock, called tectonic plates, which float on semi-liquid rocks many miles beneath the surface. As the semi-liquid matter deep in the earth circulates, it drags the tectonic plates across the earth's surface, causing the continents to move at a slow rate of only a few inches a year. Over millions of years, this movement can cause the map of the world to change dramatically.

1. Cambrian (530 mya*)

* mya = million years ago

2. Devonian (385 mya)

3. Permian (265 mya)

4. Triassic (225 mya)

During the Cambrian Period, most of the continents were separated by stretches of open ocean. During the Devonian Period, the continents were drifting toward each other. By the Permian Period, they had joined to form a single vast landmass called Pangaea. During the Triassic Period, Pangaea began to break up as the northern and southern continents moved away from each other.

SETTING THE SCENE

For 150 million years, the largest and most important animals on the earth were the dinosaurs. This unique group of reptiles evolved into hundreds of different forms. Some were smaller than a modern chicken, others were as big as a house, and they came in all sizes in between. The world of the dinosaurs was very different from that of modern times. The weather was generally warmer and wetter than it is today, and sea levels were much higher. Even the map of the world was different as continents drifted across the earth's surface. It was an alien world inhabited by strange creatures.

THE FIRST DINOSAURS

The earliest fossilized dinosaur bones that have so far been found were discovered in South America. They date back about 228 million years. These fossils, which belong to saurischian dinosaurs, may have been ancestors of the theropods and the sauropods. All these creatures walked on their hind legs. That means they could run more quickly than other animals and could use their front legs to catch prey.

▲ *This illustration shows the skull of an* Eoraptor *held in a human hand.* Eoraptor *means "dawn thief," a good name for one of the first dinosaurs.*

THE SKELETON

The key to the success of the early dinosaurs can be found in their skeletons. The skeleton below belongs to a *Coelophysis*, a small theropod of the late Triassic. Its most obvious difference from other reptiles is that the *Coelophysis* stands on two legs. The long tail balances the body and the legs are tucked underneath so the animal's weight is supported by the bones. This leaves the muscles free to provide power for running. The bones often had holes or air pockets that kept them especially light. These physical adaptations all helped a fast, agile lifestyle. Early dinosaurs were able to run more swiftly and get food more skillfully than their rivals—that is how they became dominant. Although some later dinosaurs were large and bulky, they were all relatively light for their size.

Lightweight, hollow bones

Upright bipedalism

Grasping hands

Hinged ankle bone

Fused hip

Long, balancing tail

In ornithischian dinosaurs, ▶ the pubis moved so it pointed backward instead of forward, as it did in other reptiles. This allowed the animals' massive digestive organs to rest close to the legs. Plant-eating ornithischians could remain on two legs while plant-eating saurischians—the sauropods—had to move on four legs.

Saurischian dinosaurs had ▶ the three hip bones laid out like those of modern reptiles. The ilium, which joined to the backbone, was large and rounded. The pubis pointed forward to anchor leg muscles, while the ischium pointed backward to anchor more leg muscles and tail muscles.

FAMILY TREE

Dinosaurs evolved from a small group of archosaur ancestors that lived about 225 mya. Those dinosaurs divided into two major groups that had very different features, and can most easily be identified by their hip bones. Saurischian dinosaurs had hips like modern reptiles, while ornithischians had hips like modern birds. All the ornithischians were plant-eaters and had a beaklike feature at the front of the jaw called the predentary bone. Ornithischians were fairly rare until the late Jurassic, when they evolved into new forms and became more numerous. Saurischians include the gigantic plant-eating sauropods and the meat-eating theropods.

SAURISCHIAN AND ORNITHISCHIAN

All dinosaurs are either saurischian or ornithischian. For many years, it was not clear how the two groups were related. We now know that saurischian dinosaurs evolved first. They appeared in South America about 228 mya and spread rapidly to all parts of the world. Then, about 210 mya, a small group of dinosaurs evolved in southern Africa. These plant-eaters developed a beaklike feature at the front of their jaws. The layout of their hip bones also evolved to make room for a larger digestive system that could extract as much nutrition as possible from plant food. These were the ornithischians. Unlike saurischians, these dinosaurs did not spread rapidly. They remained rare for 60 million years, until they began to develop into many new kinds of creatures in late Jurassic times.

HERRERASAURUS

Herrerasaurus was the largest, most powerful hunter of its day. It was capable of killing and eating virtually every other animal alive at the time. It had a large mouth with very sharp teeth that curved backward to give it a firm grip on its prey. Its front legs carried sharp claws that gripped a victim while the Herrerasaurus attacked with its teeth. The hind legs were powerful, which let the animal move at great speed to overtake and capture almost any creature.

PERMIAN	TRIASSIC	JURASSIC	CRETACEOUS	
			COELUROSAURS	Theropoda
			ORNITHOMIMOSAURS	
			OVIRAPTOSAURS	
			MISCELLANEOUS THEROPODS	
			SAURORNITHOIDIDS	
			DROMAEOSAURIDS	
		CARNOSAURS		
			TYRANNOSAURIDS	
	PROSAUROPODS		DIPLODOCIDS	SAURISCHIA Sauropodomorpha
		CAMARASAURIDS		
		BRACHIOSAURIDS		
			MISCELLANEOUS SAUROPODS	
		FABROSAURIDS AND HETERODONTOSAURIDS		ORNITHISCHIA
			HYPSILOPHODONTIDS	
			IGUANODONTIDS	
			HADROSAURIDS	
			PSITTACOSAURS	
			CERATOPIANS	
			PACHYCEPHALOSAURS	
			STEGOSAURIDS	
			NODOSAURIDS	
			ANKYLOSAURIDS	

MYA 280 270 260 250 240 230 220 210 200 190 180 170 160 150 140 130 120 110 100 90 80 70 64

The End of an Era

A *Cacops* amphibian watches a herd of plant-eating *Scutosaurus* reptiles wander across the plains. The herd is stalked by a ferocious, mammal-like reptile called *Inostrancevia*, which can kill a *Scutosaurus* with ease. The lizard-like creature in the foreground is *Millerosaurus*. All these animals are doomed to extinction. Mighty volcanoes spew out millions of cubic miles of rock, dust, and gas that will block out the sun. As the planet cools, the climate change causes 95 percent of all animal species to die out. The late Permian Period—245 mya—almost saw the end of life on the earth.

Trilobites (right) first appeared in the seas about 570 mya. They survived in various forms for 230 million years until they were wiped out by the Permian extinction.

The spiral shells of the ammonites (left) are found by the thousands in Permian rocks. Nearly all these relatives of modern squids became extinct at the end of the Permian.

LIFE IN PERMIAN SEAS

Life in the seas changed dramatically 285 mya, at the start of the Permian period. The southern polar ice cap melted, and the rise in sea levels flooded vast areas of land, creating warm, shallow seas ideal for marine life. Existing species, such as sharks, bony fish, and trilobites, increased in number and variety. New animals also appeared. Ammonites were active hunters that preyed on small creatures, while bivalve shellfish—like modern mussels and clams—appeared and became widespread. By the end of the Permian, all the major continents were joined in one landmass. The seas formed a single ocean through which sea animals could migrate. Sea animals of all areas were similar.

LIFE ON LAND

Conditions for life on land changed rapidly during the Permian. When the period began 285 mya, most areas were warm and wet. These conditions were ideal for the amphibians that had evolved about 80 million years earlier. There were some 100 different types of amphibians, most of which lived mainly on land. It is thought that these creatures, some of which were quite large, laid their eggs in water. The offspring spent their larval stages there, but lived on land as adults. During the Permian, however, the climate became drier and hotter. Because water can evaporate through amphibians' skins, they cannot survive long in dry air. They retreated to areas that remained damp. Most forms began to spend most of their time in or close to water.

▲ In the Permian Period, hunting sharks, such as Hybodus (above), became common. So did bony fish, like the Platysomus this Hybodus has in its mouth. Both groups survived the Permian extinction in small numbers.

The skeleton below belongs to the amphibian Eryops—another victim of the Permian extinction. This creature had a muscular body and a large mouth lined with sharp teeth. It probably floated in lakes and swamps and waited for prey to come within reach before dragging victims under water to drown.

THE REPTILES TAKE OVER

As the climate became drier and hotter, reptiles became more numerous. Waterproof skins and eggs that could be laid on dry land meant reptiles were better suited to dry conditions than amphibians. Synapsid reptiles were the most numerous. Hunters of the pelycosaur group became the largest, most powerful creatures. Plant-eating reptiles also became common. They tended to be squat, heavy creatures with widely splayed, slow-moving legs. In the later Permian, new reptiles, called therapsids, became common. They had longer legs and could run more quickly, though only for short bursts.

Edaphosaurus (below) was one of the reptiles that became more common in the Permian. The large flap of skin on its back was supported by long bones and may have been brightly colored for use in mating displays.

WHAT IS A MASS EXTINCTION?

At any given time, there are thousands of species of animals and plants on the earth. As time passes, some of these species die out and become extinct, while other species evolve into new forms. Over long periods of time, the number of different animals gradually increases—evolution creates new types of animals and plants faster than the older ones die out. At certain times in the earth's history, however, extinctions have taken place so quickly that evolution is overwhelmed and the total number of species falls dramatically. This is known as a mass extinction. One mass extinction took place 65 mya when dinosaurs and most other large animals were wiped out very quickly. The Permian extinction of 245 mya was even more serious and took place over a longer period of time.

THE PERMIAN EXTINCTION

The sheer scale of the Permian extinction was staggering. About half of all plant species died. In the seas, about 90 percent of animals were wiped out. On land, 98 percent of animals were driven to extinction. In some areas, only one or two types of animals survived. The Permian extinction did not take place all at once. The fossil record shows that extinctions began to snowball about 252 mya and reached catastrophic levels about 245 mya. The pattern of disaster shows that gradual changes slowly built up, pushing individual species out of existence. Each extinction affected other creatures. Eventually, entire ecosystems collapsed.

THE SURVIVORS

Devastating as the Permian extinction was, there were a few survivors. With their rivals out of the way, these species increased rapidly and evolved into many different forms. Twenty million years after the Permian extinction, many new types of animals appeared and life on the earth was well on the way to recovery.

◀ *Jellyfish (left) first appeared over 600 mya and survived the Permian extinction in large numbers.*

EXTINCTION THEORIES

Most scientists believe that a chain of events, rather than a single cause, brought about the Permian extinction. As the period came to a close, dramatic changes were taking place on earth. Vast volcanic eruptions in Asia poured massive amounts of dust and gas into the atmosphere. The dust blocked the sun's rays and caused climates across the planet to cool. Animals and plants that needed warmer conditions died. As water froze into ice caps, sea levels fell dramatically. This killed species that were adapted to shallow seas. Because the continents were pushed together in a single landmass, the effects of the seasons were greater. This killed species adapted to stable weather conditions.

▲ *The late Permian was a time of upheaval. As the land masses pushed together to form the supercontinent, Pangaea (above), many species lost their habitats as mountains arose and waterways disappeared. The cooling climate froze large amounts of water into the polar ice caps. This destroyed the vast shallow seas where many plants and animals lived.*

▶ *Plants were not as badly hit as animals of the Permian. Many survived, including the cycad (below) and gingko (right).* ▼

▼ *The dicynodont group of reptiles survived the Permian and rapidly increased in number. Soon, Lystrosaurs (below) made up 90 percent of reptiles on the southern continents.*

One dramatic theory to explain the Permian extinction is that a gigantic meteorite or comet plunged into Earth. Such a collision, it is said, would have killed all life close to the impact point. The mass of dust thrown into the atmosphere would have choked most life elsewhere on the planet. No impact crater, however, has ever been found, and rocks of the period show no sign of meteorite or comet dust.

Reptiles on Land

About 25 million years after the Permian extinction, large herds of stocky *Placerias* reptiles lumber across the landscape. They use their tough tusks to dig the ground in search of roots and tubers to eat. Some tear off leaves with their powerful, beaked jaws. High above them, swarms of *Peteinosaurus* swoop and soar in search of insects to eat. The peace is suddenly disrupted by the arrival of a *Euparkeria*, a powerful hunter with sharp, slicing teeth.

REPTILIAN EGGS

The ancestors of reptiles—amphibians—laid eggs with an amnion around the embryo that controlled the flow of gases in and out. Reptiles laid cleidoic, or "closed," eggs with a hard or leathery shell to stop the egg from drying out on land.

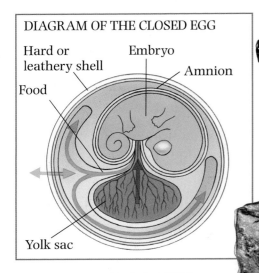

DIAGRAM OF THE CLOSED EGG

Hard or leathery shell

Embryo

Amnion

Food

Yolk sac

THE REPTILE FAMILY TREE

All reptiles belong to one of four groups. The first is the anapsids, such as turtles and tortoises, which have skulls without gaps between the bones. The second group is synapsids, which have a single opening between the skull bones. Mammals evolved from these reptiles. The third group is the diapsids, which have two skull openings. Dinosaurs and crocodiles are diapsids. The final group, the euryapsids, had an opening high on each side of the head. This extinct group included marine reptiles such as Ichthyosaurs and Plesiosaurs.

▲ *Hylonomus was about 3 feet (1 m) long. It probably hunted insects and other small creatures with its short, sharp teeth.*

THE FIRST REPTILES

About 300 mya, the earliest known reptiles lived in damp forests that covered what is now eastern Canada. These first reptiles were small and agile, but within a few million years, much larger animals had evolved. Reptiles spread rapidly across North America and Europe, but it was some time before they moved to Asia, Africa, and other continents.

THE RISE OF REPTILES

For 240 million years, reptiles dominated the world. The greatest hunters and plant-eaters on land were reptiles. The seas swarmed with predatory reptiles that ate anything in their paths. Even the skies were filled with flying reptiles. These creatures owed their success to their ability to live on dry land without returning to the water, as their ancestors, the amphibians, had to do. Free to roam the earth, reptiles evolved into many forms and took advantage of the food and lifestyles available.

THE FIRST LAND ANIMALS

About 350 mya, animals evolved that could survive out of water long enough to eat land plants. The first land animals were invertebrates with hard body shells, such as insects and the scorpion (like the fossil above).

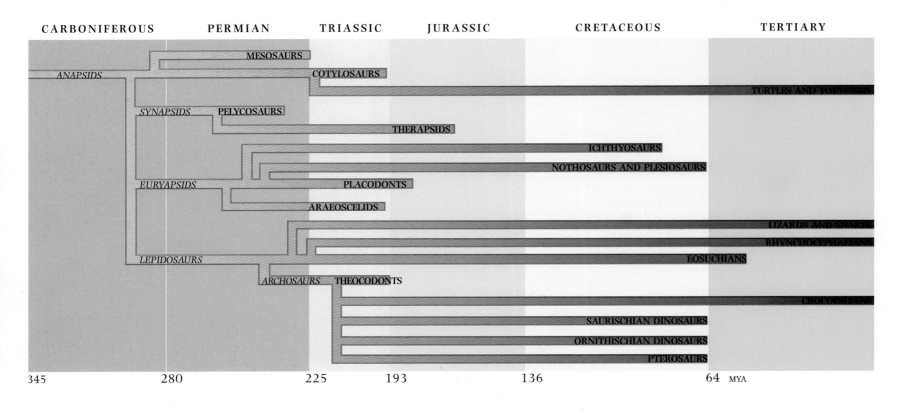

CARBONIFEROUS	PERMIAN	TRIASSIC	JURASSIC	CRETACEOUS	TERTIARY

MESOSAURS

ANAPSIDS

COTYLOSAURS

TURTLES AND TORTOISES

SYNAPSIDS   PELYCOSAURS

THERAPSIDS

ICHTHYOSAURS

NOTHOSAURS AND PLESIOSAURS

EURYAPSIDS   PLACODONTS

ARAEOSCELIDS

LIZARDS AND SNAKES

RHYNCHOCEPHALIANS

LEPIDOSAURS

EOSUCHIANS

ARCHOSAURS   THECODONTS

CROCODILIANS

SAURISCHIAN DINOSAURS

ORNITHISCHIAN DINOSAURS

PTEROSAURS

345   280   225   193   136   64 MYA

MAMMAL-LIKE REPTILES

During the Permian Period, from 286 to 245 mya, the most successful reptiles were the synapsids. These reptiles gradually evolved mammal-like features such as strong jaws, teeth with different shapes, and hair. They also kept some reptile traits, such as laying eggs. The fossilized eggs (left) were laid about 260 mya in southern Africa.

▲ Rhynchosaurus *had sprawling legs, a thick body, and beaklike front teeth.*

RHYNCHOSAURS

During the Triassic Period, 248 to 206 mya, plant-eating diapsid reptiles known as rhynchosaurs lived in the southern continents. The different types all had large, stocky bodies and strong, muscular legs. Their front teeth were used to grasp the fronds of seed ferns, which grew in vast numbers at the time. The leaves were then chopped up by rows of interlocking rear teeth. About 215 mya, the seed ferns died out, and the rhynchosaurs also became extinct.

THECODONTS

About 230 mya, a new reptile appeared—the thecodont. Thecodonts, whose name means "socket-tooth," were diapsids. The earliest thecodonts lived in swampy areas and had the ability to push themselves along with their powerful hind legs. Later thecodonts moved to dry land and were able to run for short distances on their hind legs alone, which made them much quicker than other reptiles. These creatures later evolved into dinosaurs.

▲ Erythrosuchus *was a typical large thecodont hunter. It lived in the early Triassic period in Africa and grew to be 15 feet (4.5 m) long.*

BACK TO THE WATER

Having developed to live on land, some reptiles soon evolved to live in the water. There was plenty to eat in the water, and reptiles could use their powerful legs and tails to swim.

WHAT IS A REPTILE?

Reptiles are among the most successful animals that have ever lived. They first evolved about 300 mya and quickly became the most important form of life on land. As some evolved, they were able to live in the sea and to fly. Reptiles were successful because they were well adapted to life on land. They had strong legs to support their weight and waterproof skins that kept their bodies from drying out. They also laid eggs that could survive on land, unlike amphibians, which had to lay their soft eggs in water. Reptiles absorbed heat from their surroundings, often from sunshine, to warm their bodies. Only when they were warm enough could they move quickly and effectively. Later reptiles evolved into mammals and birds that can create their own body heat. Although these new groups have taken over the land and the skies, there are still hundreds of different reptile species alive today.

REPTILES IN THE AIR

While the reptiles were evolving to take over the ground, the air belonged to the insects that had evolved to live on land long before the reptiles. Any reptile that could take to the air would not only be able to escape from danger, but could also hunt insects without competition. One of the first reptiles to evolve to do this was Icarosaurus (above), which lived in North America about 220 mya. It had very long ribs that were linked by a flap of skin. It could not actually fly, but was able to glide from tree to tree for as far as 200 feet (60 m) without landing.

◀ *In the later Triassic period, about 215 mya,* Henodus *evolved to feed on shellfish. It had a square jaw filled with broad, crushing teeth. It was 3 feet (1m) long, and its back and underside were covered in thick plates of bone and horn to protect it from hunters.*

The First Dinosaurs

A pack of hungry *Coelophysis* snap at anything that moves on the arid lands of late Triassic North America, where months of heavy rain were followed by long summers of dry heat. The ferocious, agile, and powerful *Coelophysis* survived the annual droughts by preying on anything it could find. A pack of these predators could bring down even the largest animal of the time.

ARCHOSAUR CHARACTERISTICS

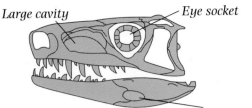

Large cavity — Eye socket

EUPARKERIA SKULL — Jaw cavity

The skull of the early archosaur *Euparkeria* (above), shows some characteristic archosaur traits. In front of the eye is a large cavity. A smaller one is found on the lower jaw. These cavities may have held glands, perhaps to secrete salt. The skeleton of *Saurosuchus* (right) shows other distinct features, including a row of bony plates in the skin of the back, a long tail, and semi-erect posture.The rear legs were stronger and longer than the front legs.

THE DAWN OF DINOSAURS

The emergence of the dinosaurs as the most important land animals took place over several million years. They developed from a hugely successful group of reptiles, the archosaurs, which appeared in the late Permian Period. In the Triassic, archosaurs became the leading hunters on land. One small group of archosaurs evolved special features in the skull and the way they walked. There may also have been other new features, such as an improved heart and metabolism, which are not seen in fossils. These changes made them dinosaurs, and they gradually became the most numerous and important animals on the earth.

Bony plates

Rear legs longer than front legs

Long tail

SAUROSUCHUS SKELETON

POSTURE

All early reptiles had legs that stuck out sideways from their bodies—a posture they inherited from their amphibian ancestors and which most modern reptiles still have. The stance is suited to small animals but makes movement slow. Animals that needed to run quickly to escape danger or catch prey evolved to have a more upright stance for greater speed. Eventually, some animals evolved a fully upright stance. This gave them speed and allowed them to grow larger because their weight was carried by the bones, not the muscles.

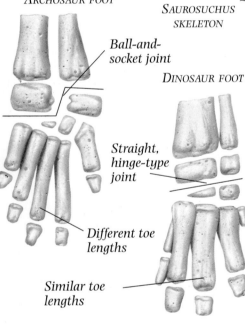

ARCHOSAUR FOOT

Ball-and-socket joint

DINOSAUR FOOT

Straight, hinge-type joint

Different toe lengths

Similar toe lengths

▲ *Most reptiles, like this Proterosuchus, have a sprawling posture with the upper legs sticking out sideways from the body.*

◄ *A few reptiles, such as Euparkeria (left), were able to pull their legs partly under their body when running. This is the semi-erect posture.*

ARCHOSAUR ANKLES

The change from the semi-erect posture of the archosaurs to the fully erect posture of the dinosaurs involved major changes to the ankle joint and foot. Because the archosaur foot was partly to the animal's side, the ankle joint had to be able to twist as the body moved past the foot. This meant that the archosaurs had a ball-and-socket joint in the ankle. The dinosaur ankle, however, only had to bend backward and forward as the body moved over it, so the ball-and-socket joint vanished. Another key difference is that dinosaur toes were all about the same length, whereas archosaur toes were of different lengths, to cope with the twisting movement.

► *The direct ancestors of dinosaurs, like this Ornithosuchus (right) had a fully erect posture with the legs directly beneath the body. This posture is shared only by mammals and birds.*

First Dinosaurs 18 • First Pterosaurs 28 • Mammals and Dinosaurs 31

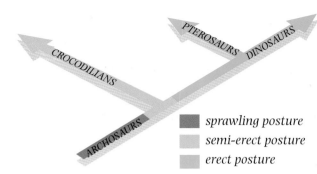

CROCODILIANS
PTEROSAURS DINOSAURS
ARCHOSAURS

sprawling posture
semi-erect posture
erect posture

THEROPODS

The first dinosaurs were the saurischians, which quickly divided into two groups. The first of these was the theropods, meat-eating predators that walked on two legs. For the next 160 million years, the largest hunters on land were theropods. Theropods had large heads with powerful jaws and sharp, usually curved teeth. The front limbs were strong enough to grip prey, and the hind legs often had large claws to kick victims.

This fossil skeleton is of a Coelophysis that lived in North America in the late Triassic. This dinosaur was typical of smaller theropods, being about 10 feet (3 m) long. The bones were thin and hollow (the name coelophysis means "hollow form"). It was a swift hunter. The long neck was able to dart from side to side in search of small prey.

THE ARCHOSAURS SPLIT

Toward the middle of the Triassic, archosaurs divided into three types of reptiles. The first, which were the ancestors of modern crocodiles and alligators, appeared about 235 mya. The second type was the pterosaurs, or flying reptiles, which probably evolved slightly earlier than 227 mya. The third group was the dinosaurs. Having evolved into these three groups, the archosaurs themselves died out by the end of the Triassic.

This Herrerasaurus skeleton is about the same length as Coelophysis, but it has features typical of larger theropods. The skull was long and deep, which allowed powerful muscles to close the jaw with a snap. The jaw itself had a hinge to give a secure grip. The front legs were robust and could exert a powerful grip. The animal was built to kill and eat fairly large animals.

The Riojasaurus (below) was one of the largest prosauropods. It grew to be 33 feet (10 m) long and had a large, stocky body set on solid legs shaped like pillars. Only slightly larger than Plateosaurus, it was much heavier and probably always walked on all four legs. These dinosaurs were probably the most important plant-eaters of their time.

PROSAUROPODS

The second large group of saurischians were the sauropodomorphs, which included the largest dinosaurs. The first to appear were the prosauropods, which developed in the late Triassic and survived into the early Jurassic. The prosauropods probably evolved from early theropods that stopped hunting in favor of the less demanding plant-eating lifestyle. They may have first appeared in southern Africa about 210 mya, but spread quickly across the globe.

Plateosaurus grew to be about 23 feet (7 m) long, but almost half this length was its tail. The long, heavy tail balanced the front part of the body and probably helped Plateosaurus rear up and run *on its hind legs.*

Danger in the Triassic

A hungry *Postosuchus* watches a herd of *Placerias* lumber by. *Postosuchus* is the largest Triassic meat-eater. It feeds on a variety of creatures, including the mammal-like reptiles that are so common. Even though it is fast and powerful, the *Postosuchus* does not dare attack the solidly built *Placerias*. It has learned how lethal their cheek horns can be, and will only attack a lone *Placerias* when it can surprise the prey.

SLOW-MOVING BUT LETHAL

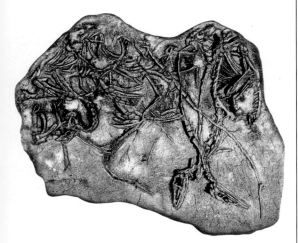

Fossils are the remains of animals preserved in rocks. Usually, single animals are found, and often only parts of an animal. Sometimes, however, vast numbers of animals are found all together. At the Ghost Ranch site in New Mexico, dozens of *Coelophysis* skeletons were found piled on top of each other. A sudden flood probably drowned and buried a pack of these creatures. Dramatic as such events may be, they do not explain species extinctions. There are usually some survivors of any flood or drought. Environmental changes, such as those that caused the Permian extinction, are more devastating. Sometime in the mid-Triassic, many groups of reptiles died out and were replaced by dinosaurs. The dinosaurs may have taken over because they were better adapted to the dry conditions of the time. Some scientists believe, however, that a giant meteorite hit Canada about this time and caused massive climatic changes that killed off many other reptiles.

PLACERIAS
One of the most common plant-eaters of the later Triassic was the reptile *Placerias*. It grew to be 10 feet (3 m) long and and weighed around a ton. The success of *Placerias* was probably due to its teeth, which were able to move backward and forward to grind up tough plants. Although large, *Placerias* could not stop an attack by a pack of *Coelophysis*. Its only hope was to use its tusks to injure and drive off the hunters.

SURVIVAL IN THE TRIASSIC

The reign of the dinosaurs was just starting in the Triassic. The period was not dominated by any one group of animals. Instead, many creatures competed for food and resources. Several different groups of reptiles dominated on land. The most numerous in the early and mid-Triassic were mammal-like reptiles of the cynodont and dicynodont group. Later in the Triassic, diapsid reptiles became more common. These included crocodiles, pterosaurs, and dinosaurs.

◄
Dragonflies evolved many millions of years before the Triassic. They were the largest hunters of flying insects.

POSTOSUCHUS
Postosuchus was the largest, most powerful hunter of the late Triassic. It was about 20 feet (6 m) long, and could rear up on its hind legs to pounce on prey. It probably used surprise to overwhelm larger animals, such as *Placerias*, biting before the prey could react. The *Postosuchus* was related to the ancestors of crocodiles.

Rutiodon *was a typical phytosaur with a crocodile-like body and sprawling legs. The largest were about 10 feet (3 m) long.*

AGGRESSIVE CROCODILE-LIKE PREDATORS

In northern Pangaea during the late Triassic, a group of hunters called phytosaurs evolved. They were common for a few million years before dying out. They looked like crocodiles, but had extensive armor made of bone plates set in the skin. They were like crocodiles because they evolved to fit a similar lifestyle. The two groups were only distantly related.

This fossilized skull of the phytosaur Nicrosaurus *is long and slender, with small, sharp teeth. Scientists think it fed mainly on fish it caught in the rivers and lakes of the late Triassic. The nostrils are high on the skull, so it could keep its jaws under water while hunting.*

CYNODONTS

Among the hunters of the Triassic were the cynodonts. These creatures first appeared in the late Permian and survived until the late Triassic. The name *cynodont* means "dog-tooth" and refers to the teeth. The cynodonts are called mammal-like reptiles. They share some features with mammals. In the late Triassic, the cynodonts evolved to become mammals.

Unlike other reptiles, Cynognathus *had a covering of fur that helped it maintain a steady body temperature. This animal grew to be about 3 feet (1 m) long.*

The Cynognathus *skull shows the long canine teeth near the front of its mouth. These teeth are found only in mammals and their ancestors, the cynodont group of mammal-like reptiles.*

CANNIBALISM

It is unusual for animals to eat other members of the same species. Even the most ferocious hunters avoid cannibalism, preferring to feed on plant-eaters. In 1947, scientists found the fossils of adult *Coelophysis* with bones of baby *Coelophysis* inside them. At first, it seemed that these dinosaurs had given birth to live young instead of laying eggs. Later study, however, showed that the baby *Coelophysis* were not complete skeletons, but parts of bodies. Undoubtedly, they were the last meal of the adult *Coelophysis* before they died. Perhaps the *Coelophysis* ate anything it could catch, even its own babies. Some scientists, however, suggest that the adult may have been injured in some way and unable to catch its normal prey. It may have been so hungry that it was driven to devour its own young before it eventually died.

Reptiles in the Air
A pair of *Eudimorphodon* swoop over a river in search of food in late Triassic Europe. This reptile's teeth show that its main food was fish, caught by plunging its jaws into the water as it flew just above the surface. The juvenile *Eudimorphodon* may have hunted insects, since it was not large enough to carry a fish. These pterosaurs, which lived about 220 mya, are among the earliest yet discovered.

GLIDING

Staying in the air is difficult. The easiest way is to glide, which is simply a way to slow down the rate at which a body falls. This is best performed by animals with a large surface area compared to their weight. Most gliding animals have large flaps of skin for surface area. Gliding uses no muscles, so powered flight is not possible.

KUEHNEOSAURUS

In late Triassic Europe, the *Kuehneosaurus* was a very efficient glider. It could probably glide for 200 feet (60 m), while losing only 6 feet (2 m) in height. The flap of skin that allowed this was supported by extended ribs that stuck out from the sides of the body. *Kuehneosaurus* probably lived in trees and glided from one tree to another to escape danger.

SHAROVIPTERYX

Living in central Asia in the late Triassic, *Sharovipteryx* had extremely long hind legs with a flap of skin connected to the tail and body. The front legs were much shorter and ended in tiny claws. It is possible that *Sharovipteryx* ran along the ground, then leapt into the air and glided forward, using its front legs to grab insects.

THE FIRST PTEROSAURS

For millions of years, the only animals that could fly were insects. The largest flying insects were dragonflies—hunters that ruled the skies as they preyed upon smaller insects. From time to time, a few reptiles evolved the power to glide short distances. Then, in the Triassic Period, an entirely new type of animal evolved—the pterosaurs. Their name means "wing-reptiles." They were able to fly, not just glide, and could hunt insects in the air or snap up fish from lakes and seas. For millions of years, the skies were ruled by the pterosaurs, until the birds took over.

Next, flaps of skin evolved between the front and hind legs for use in gliding.

The ancestor of the pterosaurs would have been a small, four-legged reptile that lived in trees.

The next feature would have been long fourth fingers, to increase the area of the skin flap and make gliding more efficient.

EVOLUTION OF THE PTEROSAURS

The earliest known pterosaur fossils come from the late Triassic Period. They are fully evolved. So far, no fossils have been found of a creature that is partly evolved from a land reptile into a flying pterosaur. However, there are clues in pterosaur fossils that show how it may have evolved. The skull bones show characteristics similar to a group of early reptiles called eosuchians from the late Permian Period. Crocodiles and dinosaurs later evolved from this group. It is thought that a small eosuchian adapted to climbing trees, then evolved into a gliding animal, from which the pterosaurs then developed. However, scientists do not know the precise details of pterosaur evolution.

An animal with true wings that came from the front legs, and with more powerful muscles to pull the wing down and allow powered flight, would have been the last step before the pterosaur.

PETEINOSAURUS

Living in Europe around 220 mya, *Peteinosaurus* flew alongside *Eudimorphodon*, but was smaller, at about 2 feet (60 cm) in wingspan. It had many short, sharp teeth ideal for snapping at insects, which it probably caught while it flew. The wings were short in proportion to its body.

The foot of Peteinosaurus *is unique. It has a long fifth toe with no claw. Nobody is certain what this toe's purpose was.*

THE PTEROSAUR BODY PLAN

All pterosaurs shared a common body plan. The front legs had evolved into specialized wings. The fourth finger was extremely long and supported most of the wing. The arm was short and connected by powerful muscles to a very large breastbone. These muscles flapped the wings and kept the creature airborne. Three of the fingers had small claws. A small outgrowth from the wrist bones supported a flap of skin in front of the wing and may have been used at low speeds. The rear legs were relatively short and slender. Some pterosaurs may have been able to walk upright on their hind legs, but most probably crawled on all fours. Early Triassic pterosaurs tended to have shorter wings and longer hind legs than later types. These characteristics may indicate that the pterosaur body plan was still evolving. Later pterosaurs, called *pterodactyls*, had a very short tail that hardly projected from the rear of the body.

EUDIMORPHODON

The most remarkable feature of *Eudimorphodon* is its highly specialized teeth, which can be seen in the fossil skull (above). At the front of the jaw were long, pointed fangs with gaps between them. Further back in the jaw were numerous small teeth with several points each, and a few more long fangs, all tightly packed together. In all, there were about 110 teeth in jaws just $2^{1}/_{2}$ inches (6 cm) long. It is thought the teeth were a good way to catch fish, which would have been slippery and hard to grasp.

Long tail for balance and steering

Large eyes for good vision

PREONDACTYLUS

Named after the Preone Valley in Italy where its fossils have been found, the *Preondactylus* lived about 215 mya. This small pterosaur had a wingspan of only 18 inches (45 cm) and probably fed on fish or insects. Details of the skeleton show that this creature may have been the ancestor of the *Rhamphorhynchus* group of pterosaurs that was common in the Jurassic Period.

Strong skeleton with light, hollow bones

Fused vertebrae to strengthen shoulders for flight

Wing membrane

Grasping claws, used for roosting

Wing bone and long fourth finger

This picture shows two Preondactylus, fishing and hunting for insects. These small pterosaurs had relatively long tails.

This skull of a Preondactylus shows the pointed teeth and the ring of bone that supported the eye.

■ 29

Mammals and Dinosaurs

While the powerful hunting dinosaur *Herrerasaurus* searches for prey, two tiny mammals risk an outing from the dense undergrowth where they are usually found. The long-nosed *Megazostrodon* hunted insects and other invertebrates in the leaves that covered the ground. The blunt-nosed *Haramiya* probably fed on fruits and succulent shoots. Mammals rarely came out in the daylight for fear of being snapped up as the prey of meat-eating dinosaurs.

SYNAPSIDS

The distant ancestor of mammal-like reptiles and mammals themselves was a small reptile that lived in the Carboniferous Period about 300 mya. The skull of this reptile had two large openings in the bones behind and below the eyes. This feature allowed powerful muscles to attach to the jaws, which gave this reptile a strong bite. As these reptiles evolved, the jaws grew even stronger and were equipped with special teeth for processing food efficiently.

PELYCOSAURS

By the start of the Permian Period, 290 mya, synapsid reptiles evolved into a group called as pelycosaurs. These animals had the sprawling posture of reptiles, but had teeth of different shapes and sizes, like modern mammals. These reptiles were very successful. By 270 mya, about 70 percent of all reptiles were pelycosaurs.

One of the largest pelycosaurs was Dimetrodon, *a hunting reptile from North America that lived about 270 mya. It was about 10 feet (3 m) long, and had a large sail of skin on its back, supported by bones. The sail may have absorbed heat from the sun.* ▶

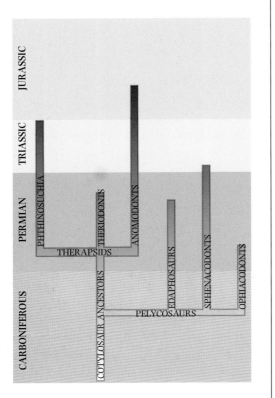

THE FIRST MAMMALS

Both dinosaurs and mammals evolved in the late Triassic Period from reptile ancestors. Dinosaurs appeared a few million years before mammals and developed rapidly to take over most habitats available to larger land animals. Mammals first evolved as insect hunters and fruit eaters that lived in dense foliage and may have been active only at night. Mammals were small and insignificant for the next 150 million years, while dinosaurs became the largest, most diverse group of animals on the earth. By getting there first, the dinosaurs took the main habitats and stopped mammals from evolving further.

▲ *The earliest known synapsid reptile is* Archaeothyris, *which lived in North America about 300 mya. It had the typical synapsid skull, but was otherwise very similar to most small reptiles of the time. The legs splayed out sideways and it had simple teeth.* Archaeothyris *was about 20 inches (50 cm) long. It probably ate insects and other invertebrates from the dense forests that covered most of the earth.*

👁 Permian Extinction 13 • Rise of Reptiles 16 • Survival in the Triassic 24

▲ *The skeleton of* Lycaenops *shows features of therapsid reptiles. It has long canine teeth and the legs are set more beneath the body, not splayed out as with most reptiles.*

THERAPSIDS

About 260 mya, the meat-eating pelycosaurs evolved to give rise to a group of reptiles known as therapsids. These creatures had larger synapsid skull openings than their pelycosaur ancestors and long canine teeth with definite structure, like later mammals. Therapsids spread rapidly to all parts of the world and evolved into a number of groups, including the plant-eating dicynodonts and the hunting cynodonts.

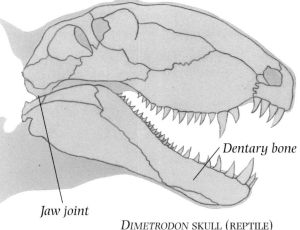

Jaw joint

DIMETRODON SKULL (REPTILE)

Dentary bone

THE EVOLUTION OF MAMMAL JAWS

A key difference between true mammals and their mammal-like reptile ancestors is found in the jaw bones. In reptiles, the lower jaw has five different bones that are often locked together, although in some reptiles they can move against each other to alter the shape of the mouth. In mammals, however, the lower jaw is made up of only one bone, the dentary. The other jaw bones moved inward, first to form part of the jaw hinge, and later, to become the delicate bones inside the ears.

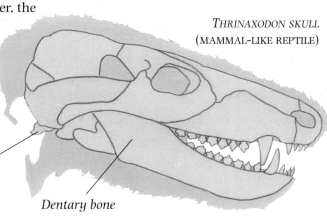

THRINAXODON SKULL
(MAMMAL-LIKE REPTILE)

Jaw joint

Dentary bone

MAMMAL CHARACTERISTICS

Mammals have some special features. One of the most important is that they give birth to live young, instead of laying eggs. Those young are suckled on milk produced by the mammary glands, which give mammals their name. Mammals have fur or hair to help keep them warm. They can produce their own heat by burning up food in their bodies, whereas reptiles have to absorb heat from their surroundings. None of these features, however, can be seen in a fossil. Instead, scientists rely on details of the jaw joint or teeth and on the structure of bones in the roof of the mouth to decide if a fossil belongs to a mammal or to a mammal-like reptile. There have been many disputes as to whether fossils from the late Triassic and early Jurassic come from true mammals or not.

WHISKERS

Pits found on the fossilized nose bones of the first mammals show that these creatures had long, sensitive hairs around the muzzle. Whiskers help animals find their way in the dark by touching objects before they bump into them. Some scientists believe whiskers mean early mammals were active at night. Others think the whiskers show they lived much of their lives in underground burrows. The creature shown here is a *Megazostrodon*, a 5 inch (12 cm) mammal from late Triassic Africa.

MAMMALS AND DINOSAURS

A *Saltopus* dinosaur prepares to eat a *Morganucodon* mammal that it has just killed. These creatures lived in Europe during the late Triassic Period, when both mammals and dinosaurs were relatively new on the earth. *Saltopus* was one of the smaller hunting dinosaurs, at only 2 feet (60 cm) long and 2 pounds (1 kg) in weight. It was fast-moving, with strong, grasping hands. It probably hunted small animals, such as mammals. Throughout the era of the dinosaurs, mammals were tiny creatures that fed on insects or fruits. They grew larger after the dinosaurs became extinct.

▼ *The fossil below is of a Thrinaxodon, a mammal-like reptile of the early Triassic. The position in which it was found is typical of small mammals when they hibernate. This may show that this creature slept through cold or very dry periods of the year.*

Beneath Triassic Waves
The dolphinlike ichthyosaur swims lazily through the shallow seas of the mid-to-late Triassic world. It has just eaten a large meal of bony fish and shrimplike creatures, so it brushes past the others. Its appetite will return later in the day. Below the ichthyosaur, a sharp-toothed nothosaurus plunges toward a coiled ammonoid that tries desperately to escape. In the background, a ferocious placodont eyes some tasty-looking fish.

TRIASSIC SEAS, RIVERS, AND LAKES

An increasing range of creatures, including coiled shellfish called ammonoids, and other mollusks, bivalves, gastropods, sea urchins, and bony fish, lived in the warm, shallow Triassic seas. The first types of modern coral also developed during the Triassic. Some animals, such as the ichthyosaurs, placodonts, and nothosaurs, led fully aquatic lives in the Triassic seas, but many others lived between water and land, or in the rivers and lakes that covered the landscape.

ICHTHYOSAURS

The origins of this dolphinlike group of marine reptiles have not yet been discovered. The earliest fossils, of the *Mixosaurus*, date to the early Triassic. They show a streamlined animal that is fishlike in shape. (The group's name means "fish-reptile.") Ichthyosaurs were totally adapted to life in the water, and could not come ashore to lay eggs. Instead, they gave birth to live young in the water. Ichthyosaurs thrived for over 100 million years, before dying out during the Cretaceous Period.

► *The Shunosaurus (right) lived in late Triassic times. It is the largest of the known ichthyosaurs. Adults measured up to 49 feet (15 m).*

THE WEIRDEST REPTILES

Scientists were astonished when they uncovered fossils of the *Tanystropheus* reptile that lived in mid-Triassic seas in Germany. These bizarre creatures grew up to 23 feet (7 m), but almost half their body length was made up of the neck. Their long necks probably helped them catch their preferred food —fish. Baby *Tanystropheus* had a neck that was in proportion to its body length. Babies probably fed on insects. By the time they reached adulthood, their necks had grown up to 12 feet (3.5 m) long.

◄ *Tanystropheus were not fully aquatic. Their fossils have been found in coastal areas. They probably used their extraordinary necks to snap up fish from rocks near the sea.*

WOODLAND LAKES

Although the Triassic landscape became drier as the period went on, there were still rivers, lakes, and wetlands. Amphibians, reptiles, and fish of various types lived there. These animals fed on fish and on the innumerable species of snails, clams, and swimming crustaceans that shared the water.

▲ *The* Metoposaurus *was an amphibian that inhabited the wetlands of Arizona. Although large and burly, it had a very casual hunting style. It would lie on the bottom of the lake and wait for food to come by, then snap it up.*

THE LATE TRIASSIC

The late Triassic was a turning point for animals on earth. The dinosaurs were not the only new group. They appeared alongside the first true mammals, the first crocodilians and pterosaurs, the first turtles, and the first sphenodons, or "wedge-toothed" reptiles, ancestors of the modern tuatara (below).

However, the dinosaurs were the most successful of the Triassic newcomers. During the last 10 million years of the period, they exploded into a variety of forms and became ready to seize the position of worldwide dominance they would hold for the next 100 million years.

ANURANS

Modern frogs and toads are part of an order known as anurans, which means "without tails." Their ancestors evolved in early Triassic times. The *Triadobatrachus* (right) lived about 240 mya in Madagascar. It was about 4 inches (10 cm) long.

TURTLES

Turtles have changed very little since they first appeared in the late Triassic. Even the earliest species had a shell into which they could withdraw for protection. This *Proganochelys* (below) is one of the first turtles. It lived in Germany and grew to about 3 feet, 3 inches (1 m) long.

TRIASSIC AMPHIBIANS

Labyrinthodonts were the earliest group of vertebrates to leave the water to live on dry land during late Devonian times. They thrived until the early Jurassic. One of the strangest members of this group was *Gerrothrax* (below). It lived in southern Germany toward the end of the Triassic.

Growing up to 3 feet, 3 ▶ inches (1 m) long, Gerrothrax had gills and a flat, armored body, with a short tail and small legs.

THE REAL AGE OF DINOSAURS BEGINS

Dinosaurs first evolved during the Triassic Period, but it was in the Jurassic Period that they took over the world. The dinosaurs' great success was due to both their own abilities and environmental factors. Dinosaurs had upright legs, which enabled them to move more efficiently than other reptiles. They probably also had internal features, such as a four-chambered heart, which helped them to survive. Not only the dinosaurs became hugely successful during the Jurassic Period. Other reptile groups, such as the flying pterosaurs and swimming plesiosaurs, also increased in size and in numbers.

LAURASIA

TETHYS SEA

GONDWANALAND

▲ *The mid-Jurassic world.*

THE SHAPE OF THINGS TO COME

At the start of the Jurassic Period, all the landmasses of the world were joined together. The dinosaurs wandered all areas, so the types of dinosaurs found in different parts of the world were similar. As the climate gradually became damper and warmer, lush vegetation grew in many regions that had previously been deserts. With plenty of food to eat and space to live in, the dinosaurs grew to enormous size and existed in large numbers.

◀ *The forests of the Jurassic were home to a variety of creatures. The largest were the sauropods, such as Diplodocus, which ate leaves. In their search for food, these plant-eaters needed to beware of powerful hunters, such as Eustreptospondylus. Much smaller animals, such as mammals, scampered in the undergrowth.*

JURASSIC SKIES

Until shortly before the Jurassic began, the only flying creatures were insects. The pterosaurs changed that. These reptiles had long wings made of a thick flap of leathery skin supported by the fourth finger of the hand. Powerful arm muscles flapped the wings and enabled the pterosaurs to fly quickly and with agility. The early pterosaurs had long tails and are known as rhamphorhyncoids.

▼ *This is the skeleton of a* Barosaurus, *a type of sauropod. It grew to be about 82 feet (25 m) long and lived at the end of the Jurassic Period.*

◀ Rhamphorhynchus *lived about 175 mya and hunted fish along the coasts of southern Europe.*

This fossilized Jurassic seed ▼ *cone came from a tree similar to the modern monkey puzzle tree.*

THE AGE OF GIANTS

Many gigantic animals lived during the Jurassic Period, so the period has become known as the "Age of Giants." The most spectacular of these animals were the dinosaurs, and of these, the largest were the sauropods. The sauropods were a family of plant-eating dinosaurs with very long necks and tails, and massive, barrel-shaped bodies supported on four thick legs. Some sauropods grew to be about 98 feet (30 m) long and may have weighed around 80 tons. They were the largest animals ever to walk on land, but they were not alone. Stegosaurs were a group of dinosaurs with large spikes and plates of bone that grew along their backs. The largest reached 30 feet (9 m) in length and weighed about 3 tons. Hunting dinosaurs grew to be over 40 feet (12 m) long and weighed over 2 tons. Although the dinosaurs lived on earth for another 60 million years after the end of the Jurassic, they never again grew to be as large as they did in the Age of Giants.

JURASSIC PLANTS

The plants the dinosaurs ate were similar to some modern plants, but there were also differences. There were fir trees then, and ferns that would look familiar to us. Plants that are rare now, such as horsetails and tree ferns, were common then, but some Jurassic plants, such as cycads, have died out completely. Flowering plants that are now common did not exist at all.

JURASSIC SEAS

During the Jurassic Period, large areas of what is now land were flooded by warm, shallow seas. These waters were rich in fish and other foods for marine reptiles to eat. As a result, several types of sea-living reptiles evolved. The most successful were the plesiosaurs. These reptiles had thick bodies with four large flippers and a muscular tail. One group of plesiosaurs, the pliosaurs, had very big heads and hunted larger animals.

▲ *The* Liopleurodon *was a pliosaur that grew to be 40 feet (12 m) long. Despite its size, it was an agile swimmer and could change direction quickly as it hunted.*

Prosauropods

At the dawn of the Jurassic Period, the most numerous dinosaurs were the prosauropods. Some were little larger than a modern sheep, but others were up to 40 feet (12 m) long. They all ate plants and used their long necks to get leaves other creatures could not reach. By about 185 mya, the prosauropods had become extinct, and other plant-eating dinosaurs had taken over.

SAUROPODOMORPHS

For over 150 million years, the sauropodomorphs were the largest land animals on the earth. There were many different types, but they all belonged to one of two groups. The prosauropods appeared in the late Triassic Period and had spread across the world by the start of the Jurassic. These dinosaurs were plant-eaters with long necks and tails. Within a few million years, however, the prosauropods had died out and been replaced by the sauropods. These dinosaurs were much larger, but had long necks and tails like prosauropods.

PROSAUROPODA ► ● PLATEOSAURIADE

SAUROPODOMORPHA ►

● BRACHIOSAURIDAE

● CAMARASAURIDAE

SAUROPODA ► ● CETIOSAURIDAE

● DIPLODOCIDAE

● TITANOSAURIDAE

▲
The family tree of the sauropodomorphs divided in two about 210 mya. It is not clear if the sauropods evolved from a type of prosauropod or if the two groups shared a common ancestor.

◄ *This is the skeleton of a* Massospondylus.

THE EARLY JURASSIC

The early Jurassic Period was a time of change. Many reptiles that had been common in the Triassic were now extinct and had been replaced by dinosaurs. Various types of dinosaurs evolved rapidly as new types appeared and old ones died out. Throughout the first few million years of the Jurassic, dinosaurs tended to become larger and heavier. By the mid-Jurassic, the dinosaurs had evolved to become the largest animals ever to walk the earth.

ANCHISAURUS

This dinosaur lived in North America at the very beginning of the Jurassic Period. It was only about 8 feet (2.5 m) long and walked on all fours most of the time. It could run on its hind legs when it needed to move quickly, to escape predators, for example. If it could not run away, it had large claws on its front feet with which to defend itself.

▲ Anchisaurus *could run on its hind legs for short distances.*

► *Thecodontosaurus was one of the first dinosaurs to be discovered. Its fossils were dug up in England in 1843.*

THECODONTOSAURUS

Similar to *Anchisaurus* in many ways, *Thecodontosaurus* lived in Europe at about the same time *Anchisaurus* lived in North America. This dinosaur had a relatively short neck and more teeth than other prosauropods. This creature probably lived in dry, hilly, or mountainous areas where it foraged for plants.

MASSOSPONDYLUS

Living in Africa and North America, this was one of the most widespread of all prosauropods. Its remains are also those found most often. More than 80 fossils have been dug up by scientists. *Massospondylus* grew to be about 13 feet (4 m) long, but had a tiny head that was smaller in proportion to its body than that of other prosauropods. Its front feet had large claws and may have been used both to grasp food and to walk.

The Real Age of Dinosaurs Begins 38 • Jurassic Giants 45 • Inside a *sauropod* 50 • Stegosaurus 64

◀ Diplodocus *and* Brachiosaurus *would tower over a modern giraffe and were huge compared to the size of a human.*

▼ Massospondylus *was long and thin, with a body about the same size as that of a human.*

SIZE VARIATIONS

The early dinosaurs varied greatly in size, as can be seen here when they are compared to a modern human and modern giraffe. The smaller of these dinosaurs were among the lightest and shortest of all dinosaurs, but the larger ones were among the largest animals ever to have lived.

▲ Scutellosaurus, Lesothosaurus, *and* Thecodontosaurus *were all about the size of a small dog.*

▲ Plateosaurus *was large and solid, but* Anchisaurus *was low-slung and slender.*

ORNITHISCHIANS

Most of the very early dinosaur fossils found so far belong to the saurischian group, which means they had hips shaped like those of modern lizards. Only toward the end of the Jurassic Period did ornithischian dinosaurs, those with hips shaped like those of modern birds, become more common. Still, there were some ornithischian dinosaurs even in the earliest Jurassic. These were the fabrosaurids that lived across Africa, Asia, Europe, and the Americas. They tended to be quite small, less than half the height of a modern human, and were fast movers. They could walk on all fours but, except for *Scutellosaurus*, most probably walked on their hind legs and used their front feet to grasp food. The teeth were small and shaped like a tree leaf, with razor-sharp edges. These teeth were used to shred food into small pieces before it was swallowed and digested. These small dinosaurs later evolved into a wide variety of creatures of different sizes.

SCUTELLOSAURUS

This 4-foot (1.2-m) long creature from North America was unique among early dinosaurs because it had bone armor across its back. The bone studs were set in the skin and arranged in rows that ran from the shoulders to the hips. Like all ornithischians, *Scutellosaurus* chopped up plants with its teeth before it swallowed.

LESOTHOSAURUS

Named after the country in Africa where its fossils have been found, *Lesothosaurus* was common on the hot, dry plains that covered the area at that time. It had long, powerful hind legs to help it run very quickly, and a stout, strong tail that was used as a counterbalance to enable the dinosaur to change direction quickly. The neck was very flexible, and was able to twist the head around to search for tasty leaves and shoots.

Jurassic Giants

Giants walked the earth in the Jurassic Period. The mighty sauropod dinosaurs, such as *Diplodocus*, *Brachiosaurus*, and *Barosaurus*, were the largest land animals that ever lived. Some weighed as much as a dozen elephants and towered high into the air.

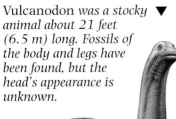

Vulcanodon *was a stocky ▼ animal about 21 feet (6.5 m) long. Fossils of the body and legs have been found, but the head's appearance is unknown.*

PRIMITIVE SAUROPOD

One of the earliest sauropods yet found is *Vulcanodon* from Zimbabwe. It lived about 185 mya. This dinosaur had hips like those of a prosauropod, but had legs and a backbone more like those of a sauropod. Although it is not clearly either a sauropod or a prosauropod, *Vulcanodon* gives us a good idea of what the earliest sauropods looked like.

JURASSIC HERBIVORES

Throughout the Jurassic Period, the land was covered with warm, lush forests and plains. Plants grew in abundance and provided vast amounts of food for the herbivores that fed on them. The largest and most numerous of these were the sauropod dinosaurs. The sauropod group is divided into a number of families, each of which contains several different creatures that share certain features. The brachiosaurids, for instance, had front legs that were longer than the back legs. Some other herbivores belonged to the ornithischian group of dinosaurs, but they were much smaller and less numerous throughout the Jurassic.

A PANORAMA OF JURASSIC HERBIVORES

Sauropods lived all over world, and their fossils have been found on every continent. They even lived on Antarctica, which was then a land of rich vegetation, not the icy wilderness it is today. Although slightly different types of sauropods were found in different areas, the main families were found on every continent.

▲ Camarasaurus *could move its neck up and down, but not side to side.*

CAMARASAURUS (CHAMBERED LIZARD)

Family: Camarasaurid
Lived: 140 mya
Location: North America
Length: 59 feet (18 m)
Weight: 20 tons
Distinguishing features:
Very large claw on the front foot, perhaps used to dig for food.

BRACHIOSAURUS (ARM LIZARD)

Family: Brachiosaurid
Lived: 150 mya
Location: East Africa and North America
Length: 40 feet (22.5 m)
Weight: 50 tons
Distinguishing features:
Large teeth shaped like chisels.

DIPLODOCUS (DOUBLE BEAM)

Family: Diplodocid
Lived: 145 mya
Location: North America
Length: 88 feet (27 m)
Weight: 10-12 tons
Distinguishing features:
Nostrils located on top of the skull, between the eyes.

CETIOSAURUS (WHALE LIZARD)

Family: Cetiosaurid
Lived: 160 mya
Location: Europe
Length: 59 feet (18 m)
Weight: 10 tons
Distinguishing features:
A relatively short neck.

The Real Age of Dinosaurs Begins 38 • Prosauropods 40 • Inside a *sauropod* 50 • Feeding on the Giants 49

ADRYOSAURUS

This dinosaur belonged to the hypsilophodont family of ornithopods. It was only about 11 feet (3.5 m) long, but could run extremely quickly on its long, slim hind legs. The front legs ended in five short fingers that may have been used to grasp food. There were no teeth at the front of the mouth, but there may have been a beak used to nip off leaves from plants.

OTHER MID- TO LATE-JURASSIC HERBIVORES

Although sauropods were the largest and most numerous Jurassic herbivores, they were not alone. A number of other plant-eaters were ornithischian dinosaurs and belonged to a group known as ornithopods, which meant "bird-foot." These dinosaurs walked on their hind legs and left footprints that look like those of modern birds, with three toes, each of which ends in a small claw.

Grinding molars

Small, sharp teeth

CAMPTOSAURUS

This medium-sized dinosaur was the first of a group that would later become extremely numerous—the iguanodontids. *Camptosaurus* was about 20 feet (6 m) long and weighed up to 4 tons. It lived in Europe and North America about 145 mya, at the very end of the Jurassic Period. This dinosaur used its front legs for support when it squatted down to eat ground plants, but otherwise it walked on its hind legs.

MAMENCHISAURUS (LIZARD FROM MAMENCH)

Family: Diplodocid
Lived: 150 mya
Location: Central Asia
Length: 72 feet (22 m)
Weight: 17 tons
Distinguishing features: Each neck bone twice as long as similar bones in the back or tail.

HETERODONTOSAURUS

This dinosaur was only about 4 feet (1.2 m) long and belonged to the fabrosaurid family. The name means "lizard with mixed teeth," which refers to the variously shaped teeth in its jaws. At the front were small, sharp teeth to nip leaves off plants; at the back were broad teeth to grind leaves into pulp. In between were long, sharp tusks, weapons that may have been used to drive off hunting dinosaurs, or perhaps to fight rival heterodontosaurs.

▲ *Mamenchisaurus had the longest neck of any known dinosaur.*

Apatosaurus was once known as Brontosaurus *—the Thunder Lizard.* ▶

BAROSAURUS (HEAVY LIZARD)

Family: Diplodocid
Lived: 145 mya
Location: North America
Length: 82 feet (25 m)
Weight: 17 tons
Distinguishing features: Bones in tail shorter than normal.

APATOSAURUS (DECEPTIVE LIZARD)

Family: Diplodocid
Lived: 145 mya
Location: North America
Length: 70-90 feet (21-27 m)
Weight: 35 tons
Distinguishing features: Teeth shaped like long, straight pegs.

◀ *Barosaurus was similar to* Diplodocus, *and some scientists think they were slightly different versions of the same animal.*

Feeding on the Giants

Packs of powerful, hungry predators hunted the gigantic sauropods across the Jurassic landscape. Equipped with terrifyingly sharp teeth and claws, these monsters could bring down a sauropod and gobble it up within hours. In the shadows lurked plenty of smaller hunters, who waited to snap up a young sauropod or to feast on the leftovers from a kill made by a larger predator.

INSIDE A SAUROPOD

The sauropods were massive creatures. Their sheer size made it hard for their bodies to function efficiently. To carry so much weight was perhaps the most obvious problem that such a large land animal would encounter, but it was also difficult to find enough food to sustain such a mass of flesh and to have a heart strong enough to pump blood all the way around the body. The sauropods evolved gradually over millions of years from much smaller animals. As their bodies grew, they managed to solve the problems caused by their size in a number of ingenious ways.

▲ The large front claw may have been used to fight off attacking hunters. It may also have been used to dig holes in which to lay eggs.

◄ *The structure of a sauropod was similar to that of a modern suspension bridge. Extremely strong tendons that ran over the back connected the neck to the tail and allowed them to balance each other, much as the cables of a bridge balance the weight of a roadway.*

The feet of sauropods tend to be fairly similar. They were wide and stout to carry the enormous weight of the animal. Most sauropods had a large, sharp claw on the front feet. ◄

THE BIOMECHANICS OF LARGE DINOSAURS

The key to understanding the structure of sauropods and other large animals is to realize that as a body doubles in height, it quadruples in weight. To support this massive weight, the legs of a large animal need to be much thicker and stronger in proportion to its height than those of a small animal. The legs of sauropods were massive. They were pillars of strong, solid bone. Sauropods probably lifted only one foot at a time so that the weight of the animal always rested on three legs.

◄ *This scientist is not even half as tall as the sauropod leg he is reconstructing.*

THE SKELETON

This *Brachiosaurus* skeleton shows that everything about the sauropod was massive. The legs were solid enough to carry the weight. The rib cage was broad and deep to allow space for the stomach and intestines needed to process large amounts of vegetable food. The tail was long to counterbalance the weight of the head and neck. Because of their vast size, sauropod skeletons were fossilized more often than those of small, delicate animals. Still, it is rare for an entire skeleton to be found. Scientists usually use parts of several skeletons to put together a complete animal.

Sauropod heads were startlingly small. As a result, the brains of these animals were very small compared to the size of the body. Some people believe this means dinosaurs were stupid, but it is more likely that nerve clusters throughout the body handled the automatic movements of various organs.

FOOD AND DIGESTION

Large animals have to process large amounts of food to get enough energy and nutrients for their bodies to function. Plants can be very tough to break down enough to extract the nutrition they contain. To solve this problem, some animals chew plant food until it is reduced to an easily digested mush. Sauropods, however, had very small jaws and could not take large mouthfuls of food. If they were to collect enough food, they had to take a bite of foliage and swallow it at once in order to move on to the next mouthful. It was impossible to chew for a long time.

DEFENSE

Adult sauropods were big and powerful enough to protect themselves from attack. They could use their sheer size to make a hunter flee. The giant plant-eaters were not without weapons, however. *Diplodocus* and some others had very long, muscular tails that could swing from side to side so quickly that the tip broke the sound barrier and produced a loud noise like the crack of a whip. Any hunter hit by this tail would receive a nasty injury. Some dinosaurs, such as *Shunosaurus*, took this strategy further. They had a large, heavy knob of bone with sharp spikes on the end of their tails. This was a powerful weapon that could have killed any predator that got too close. Most likely, attacking animals would try to catch young sauropods, so adults may have used their weapons to defend the young.

Rather than chew to break down their food, the sauropods used gastroliths, or stomach stones. They swallowed large numbers of stones or pebbles about 4 inches (10 cm) in size. These stayed in the stomach and churned about with the food as the stomach walls contracted. The stones pummeled the food into paste, ready to go to the intestine for digestion.

◀ *The neck bones of a Diplodocus show the features common to all sauropods. Through evolution, much of the bone has been lost, but without any serious loss of strength. This means the neck was much lighter than it looked.*

▼ *Young sauropods were vulnerable to attack by hunting dinosaurs. Perhaps only about one in 20 survived to adulthood.*

Some sauropods may have been specialized to feed on certain types of plants. For instance, the peg-like teeth of the diplodocids were arranged in the mouth like the teeth of a comb. The creature may have closed its mouth over the branch of a fir tree, then jerked its head back. The teeth would then strip the needles from the twigs.

Clash of the Titans
Two ferocious Allosaurus fight it out over the remains of a giant herbivore. Even active hunters like these could resort to scavenging if they thought it would bring an easy meal. Fossil finds in North America suggest that, like many carnivores, Allosaurus may have hunted in packs to bring down large prey. A lone Allosaurus would also have been a formidable enemy!

OPEN WIDE

Jurassic carnivores were well equipped to deal with their victims. The jaws of *Allosaurus*, shown here, were typical of many hunters, and show clever adaptation to hunting. In the normal position (right), the jaws could open and shut with enough force to kill. Special hinges within the jaw then enabled *Allosaurus* to widen the mouth (left) to allow it to tear out large chunks of its victim's flesh in a single bite. With such a mouthful of food, the jaws could not shut with great strength, but once the prey was dead, a strong bite was not needed.

DILOPHOSAURUS

The earliest of the large killers was *Dilophosaurus*, which lived in North America about 200 mya. It was 20 feet (6 m) long and had a large head with powerful jaws. The most remarkable feature of *Dilophosaurus* was the twin crest of bone that ran along the top of its head. It is thought that the crests might have been for display and that only males had them.

The Real Age of Dinosaurs Begins 38 • Prosauropods 40 • Jurassic Giants 45 • *Stegosaurus* 64

◀ *Dilophosaurus was much more lightly built than later carnivores and may have preyed upon fast-moving herbivores.*

JURASSIC CARNIVORES

The most ferocious of the Jurassic dinosaurs were the carnivores that hunted down and ate their fellow creatures. Some of these beasts were large, powerful hunters that could kill almost anything. Others were smaller and hunted lizards or mammals. A few did not kill at all, and instead searched for the carcasses of dinosaurs that had died of natural causes or had been killed by others.

ALLOSAURUS

The most powerful killer of the Jurassic was *Allosaurus*. This huge hunter grew to 40 feet (12 m) in length and may have weighed up to 3.5 tons. It lived in North America about 145 mya. *Allosaurus* was muscular and stocky, able to bring down medium-sized herbivores. It probably also hunted sauropods, though it may have been able only to bring down young or sick animals. *Allosaurus* probably used its long claws to grip victims as it bit them.

TEETH

However large or small a Jurassic carnivore may have been, they all had the same sort of teeth, which were sharply pointed and curved back at the tip. This shape enabled the teeth to slice into a victim and hold it firmly no matter how it struggled. The edges of the teeth were serrated like a steak knife to tear through flesh. Teeth were often broken in combat, so new ones grew continuously up from the jaws.

Proceratosaurus had a horn on its snout.

ORNITHOLESTES

Although *Ornitholestes* lived at about the same time and in the same place as *Allosaurus*, it was a very different type of killer. This dinosaur was only about 6 feet (2 m) long, but it was fast and nimble. *Ornitholestes* preyed upon lizards, insects, mammals, and other small creatures, including the babies of much larger dinosaurs. It may also have stolen meat from the carcasses of dinosaurs killed by *Allosaurus*.

▲ The head of *Ornitholestes* shows the colorful displays typical of Jurassic carnivores. The bump of bone on its nose is brightly colored and it has a flap of skin, supported by spines, on the back of its head. These may have been used to decide which *Ornitholestes* was leader of a pack.

▲ A fossil skull of Proceratosaurus. *As with many Jurassic carnivores, the skull is made up of light but strong bones with several openings where the bulging jaw muscles were located. The name* Proceratosaurus *means "before ceratosaurus" because this creature was similar to* Ceratosaurus, *but lived a few million years earlier. It may have been an ancestor of the later animal.*

CERATOSAURUS

This powerful hunter lived in North America about 145 mya and grew to be about 20 feet (6 m) long. It was probably able to run very quickly, though perhaps only for short distances. Scientists think this carnivore hunted the smaller, more agile herbivores of the Jurassic Period and left the big sauropods to the larger *Allosaurus*.

▲ A pack of Compsognathus *scours the countryside in search of prey.*

SKELETON

Jurassic carnivores had a similar body plan. They all walked on their hind legs, which were much longer and more muscular than the front legs. The hands had sharp claws on three or four fingers and were mounted on short but strong arms. The heads were relatively large and had powerful jaws.

Powerful jaws

Small, strong arms

Sharp claws

Long, sturdy hind legs

NATURAL BORN KILLERS

The smallest Jurassic carnivore, *Compsognathus*, was barely 3 feet (1 m) long. Quick and agile, *Compsognathus* hunted lizards, insects, and grubs in the dense undergrowth of the Jurassic forests in Europe. It had only two fingers on its hands, and probably killed with its slender jaws, which were filled with needle-sharp teeth.

Jurassic Skies

While dinosaurs dominated the land, the Jurassic skies were filled with a dazzling variety of creatures. Flying reptiles, which first appeared in the Triassic, now grew to enormous sizes. By the mid-Jurassic, birds had also taken to the air. Scientists have long been puzzled about how and why they evolved.

JURASSIC SKIES

A bird's compact skeleton, made up of light, hollow bones, is well suited to the needs of flight. ▼

Flying is a highly evolved skill, but it brings great rewards. It is easier to fly to escape from hunters than to run away, and it can be easier to see food from a height than from the ground. Flying demands wings and powerful muscles, however, as well as an extremely light body. Few creatures have these adaptations, but in the Jurassic, two groups of animals perfected the art of flight and dominated the skies. The first were pterosaurs, or flying reptiles. The second were birds. Although the pterosaurs later became extinct, birds still live on earth today.

Dimorphodon probably lived on cliffs near the ocean and preyed on fish.

EARLY BIRDS?

The oldest known birds had several features that link them to reptiles, and to dinosaurs in particular. Like many dinosaurs, birds walk on their hind legs, have flexible necks and large eyes, as well as some more complex anatomical similarities. There are also differences. Birds lack the long, bony tail of dinosaurs and have no teeth. Birds also have feathers and wings, which dinosaurs did not.

DIMORPHODON

This flying reptile lived in Europe at the very beginning of the Jurassic period and was one of the most primitive pterosaurs. It had long legs, short wings, and a long bony tail that acted as a rudder in flight. It had a wingspan of about 5 feet (1.5 m), which is fairly small for a pterosaur.

◄ *Small hunting dinosaurs were compact, but they had long, bony tails and strong arms.*

FISHING PTEROSAUR

By about 180 mya, pterosaurs had spread across the world. The *Dorygnathus* hunted for fish off the coasts of Europe and North America. To catch fish, this creature swooped low over the sea surface until it saw a likely victim. Then it plunged its jaws into the water, snapped them shut over a hapless fish, and flew off. Its long, sharp teeth that pointed forwards were ideal to secure slippery fish.

ARCHAEOPTERYX

The fossils of the earliest known bird were first discovered in Bavaria in 1861. The fossil of a reptile-like creature with wings and feathers proved that birds evolved from reptiles, but it was not clear which type of reptile had evolved into the birds. Today, most scientists believe it was a group of small hunting dinosaurs that developed feathers and the ability to fly.

▲ *The* Archaeopteryx *(fossil above) is thought to be the "missing link" between dinosaurs and birds. It has the bony tail and strong arms of a dinosaur, but the feathers and lightweight bones of a bird. Most scientists now accept that birds evolved from dinosaurs.*

▲ *The ancestor of the pterosaurs is believed to have been a small, four-legged reptile that lived in trees.*

PTEROSAUR FOOD

Scientists look at the jaws and teeth to learn what animals ate when they were alive. Most pterosaurs found so far seem to have eaten fish, but this may only be because animals that die near water are more likely to be fossilized. Pterosaurs that lived inland probably fed on insects, worms, lizards, and other small animals. Some pterosaurs would also have eaten dead animals, as vultures do today.

◄ Anurognathus (left) had sharp, pointed teeth, which means it probably ate insects that it caught as it flew.

Elongated fourth finger

Long, low skull with many openings

Hollow bones

▲ This pterodactyl (above) has a typical pterosaur skeleton. In flight, the head was held level and the legs trailed out behind. The short body provided attachments for the powerful muscles that flapped the wings.

The bodies of pterosaurs were superbly adapted for flight. They had all the necessary features, such as wings, powerful muscles, and light bones. The skulls of most pterosaurs were long and low with pointed jaws. The skull bones often had many holes and openings, which reduced the weight of the head. The bodies tended to be very short and stocky. The backbone was usually fairly large, and the individual bones were sometimes locked together so they could not move. This would have formed a solid base for the flapping wings. At the same time, the bones had plenty of holes and openings to reduce their weight. Beneath the ribs was an extremely large breastbone that was wide and flat. The very powerful wing muscles were attached to this bone, which allowed the wings to be pulled down with great force to keep the animal in the air. The tail bones varied greatly. In the Rhamphorhynchus, the tail was long and straight. In pterodactyls, it was short or almost nonexistent. The wings were formed of specialized front limbs. The arms themselves were like those of other reptiles, but were fairly slender. The fourth finger, however, was extremely long and was used to support the tough flap of leathery skin that formed the wing. All the bones in the body were hollow, to make them as light as possible without losing strength.

SORDES

Sordes fossils were the first to be found with fossilized fur. This suggests that they were warm-blooded, like modern mammals, rather than cold-blooded, like modern reptiles.

◄ This Dsungaripterus skull shows the upcurved jaws that may have been used to pull shellfish off rocks.

▼ More than 250 teeth filtered tiny animals from the water.

► The Ctenochasma (skeleton, right) had more than 250 long, narrow teeth. It stood in shallow coastal waters and strained the water through its teeth to trap tiny shrimps and other small animals, which it then swallowed.

SCAPHOGNATHUS

This pterosaur lived alongside Anurognathus. It had long jaws with sharply pointed teeth set wide apart. The tips of the jaws did not meet, however, and it is not clear what sort of animals this creature hunted.

👁 The Real Age of Dinosaurs Begins 38 • Life in the Sea 60

CRESTED PTEROSAURS

Germanodactylus (above), which lived in Germany about 150 mya, had a bony crest along the top of its skull. The crest may have been brightly colored and used to signal to other Germanodactylus during disputes or courtship. In later pterosaurs, the crests grew to be remarkably large structures.

Life in the Sea

The warm Jurassic seas were ruled by gigantic reptiles that hunted fish, shellfish, and each other. The rich waters were filled with vast numbers of fish and a wide variety of other creatures. These provided a generous source of food for the reptiles that had evolved to swim, including some of the most ferocious water beasts that ever lived.

MARINE CROCODILES

During the Jurassic, several types of crocodiles evolved fins or flippers in place of legs, while the tails became broad and flat to provide moving power. Sea crocodiles were very successful for a time in the mid-Jurassic, then suddenly died out.

The jaws of Cryptoclidus *were lined with long, thin, very sharp teeth that overlapped when the jaws were shut. They were a highly efficient trap for slippery fish.* ▼

The mighty sea reptiles of the Jurassic all evolved from types of Triassic land reptiles. Because the fossils of the earliest sea reptiles are very rare, it is not entirely clear how these animals evolved, or how they are related to each other. The ichthyosaurs seem to have evolved first, in the early Triassic, and may have descended from animals very like early lizards. By about 220 mya, the earliest ichthyosaurs had appeared. These animals had a basic fish shape, but had not yet evolved the fishtail that was common in Jurassic ichthyosaurs. The plesiosaurs evolved about 210 mya from earlier reptiles called nothosaurs. The nothosaurs had four legs, each of which had webbed toes and was clearly used to swim. The first plesiosaurs had long necks and small heads. These creatures probably hunted fish or squid, and darted their heads back and forth to snap up prey. In the mid-Jurassic, one group of plesiosaurs evolved to have large heads and short necks, and are known today as the pliosaurs. These animals hunted of larger prey, including the plesiosaurs themselves.

CRUSTACEANS

Jurassic seas were the first to see the crabs, lobsters, shrimps, and prawns that are so familiar today. All these creatures are crustaceans–animals with a hard outer skeleton and muscles and organs located within. During the Jurassic, crustaceans became more common and replaced earlier groups of similar animals that died out.

CRYPTOCLIDUS

One of the most successful plesiosaurs was *Cryptoclidus*. It lived in the shallow seas that covered most of Europe about 130 mya. At this time plesiosaurs were the most common sea reptiles, though their numbers later declined. *Cryptoclidus* was unusual in that its eyes faced upward. This may indicate that to hunt, it swam slowly along the bottom of the shallow seas until it arrived beneath a shoal of fish. Then it rose up, snapped at the fish with its jaws, and ate its fill.

The Real Age of Dinosaurs
Begins 38 • Jurassic Skies 56

LIFE IN THE SEA

During the Jurassic, the seas were much larger and more abundantly filled with life than they are today. The world was warmer and there were no ice caps at the poles to lock up vast quantities of water as ice. The result was that great areas were flooded by broad, shallow seas. These seas were brightly lit by the sunlight and kept warm because cold water from the depths could not reach them. Conditions were ideal for a wide variety of marine life.

▲ *A bowfin fish.*
This family of teleost fish emerged in the
early Jurassic and survives to this day.

MESOZOIC MARINE REVOLUTION

During the Jurassic, most fish were related to modern sharks and had skeletons made of cartilage, though a few had skeletons of bone. At the start of the Jurassic, a new type of fish evolved. These had bone skeletons combined with a new type of fin. These fins were supported by long parallel rays of bone, which gave the fish the name "teleosts," or ray-finned fish. During the Jurassic, the teleosts increased in numbers and types until they were the most numerous and important fish in the seas, as they remain today.

LIOPLEURODON

The most fearsome of the Jurassic sea reptiles was *Liopleurodon*, which cruised the shallow seas that covered England, France, and central Europe. This mighty animal grew to be over 40 feet (12 m) long, and its 8-foot (2.5-m) head had powerful jaws armed with strong, sharp teeth. Its muscular flippers were designed for long-distance swimming, so it could swim far and fast in pursuit of its prey.

ICHTHYOSAURS

The ichthyosaurs were specialized for life in the sea. They could not leave the water at all, even to lay eggs. They gave birth to live young, probably in shallow, sheltered lagoons where the young would be safe from the larger hunters of the open seas. The name "ichthyosaur" means "fish reptile" and perfectly describes the body shape of these animals.

AMMONITES

Among the most numerous creatures in the Jurassic seas were ammonites, thousands of which lived in vast shoals. These creatures were distantly related to modern squid, but they lived in a hard, coiled shell. As the ammonite grew, it built a new chamber of shell into which it moved. The old chambers were filled with gas and helped keep the animal afloat. As ammonites swam, they used their tentacles to capture small fish and other prey.

▲
We know a lot about the ichthyosaurs because of a series of fossils found in Germany, like the one shown here. These fossils preserved not only the bones, but also the muscles and skin.

MARINE PLANTS

The plants of the Jurassic seas were very like those of modern oceans. In shallow waters, large forests of kelp and algae relied on the sunlight that reached the sea floor. In deeper waters, free-floating diatoms and tiny algae drifted with the ocean current.

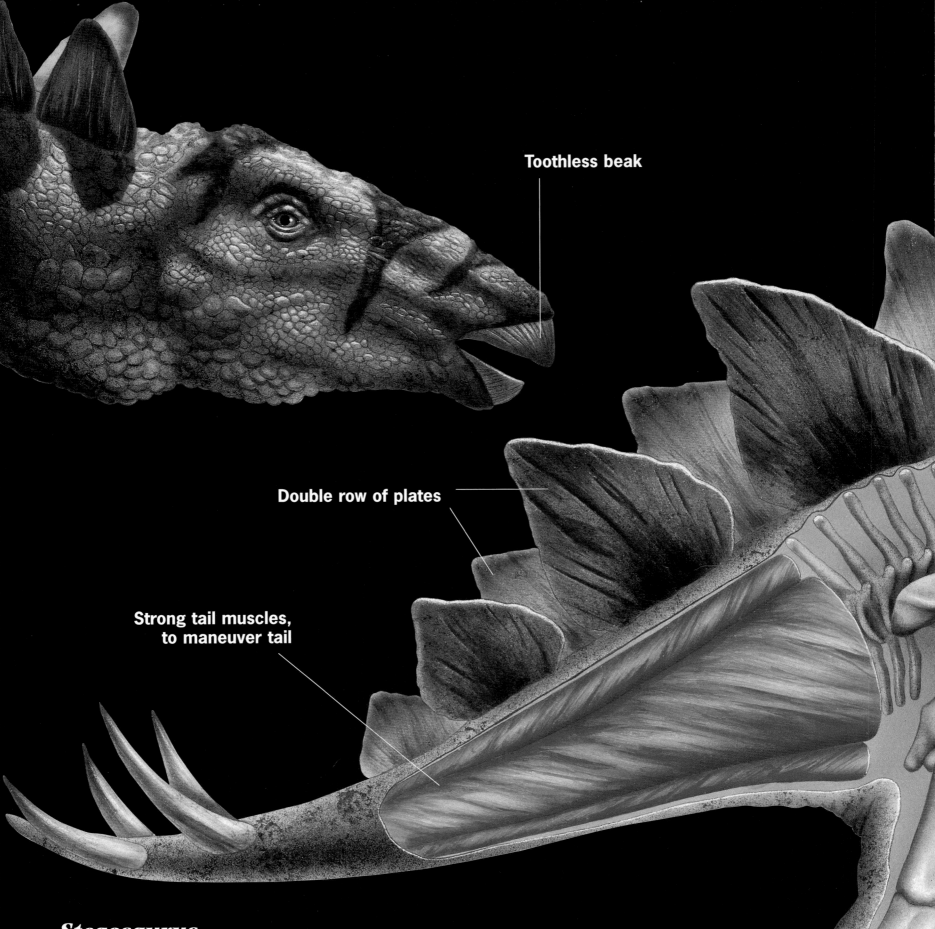

Toothless beak

Double row of plates

Strong tail muscles, to maneuver tail

Stegosaurus

The largest of the plated dinosaurs, a fully grown *stegosaurus*, or "roofed lizard," was as long as a modern bus. Like all stegosaurs, it moved on four sturdy legs, and fed on grass and leaves. Its skull, very small compared to its huge body, contained a tiny brain. *Stegosaurus's* snout ended in a toothless beak, which was probably used to crop foliage. On the end of its hefty tail, this creature carried a powerful weapon—four sharp spikes— with which it could wallop any animal that dared to attack it.

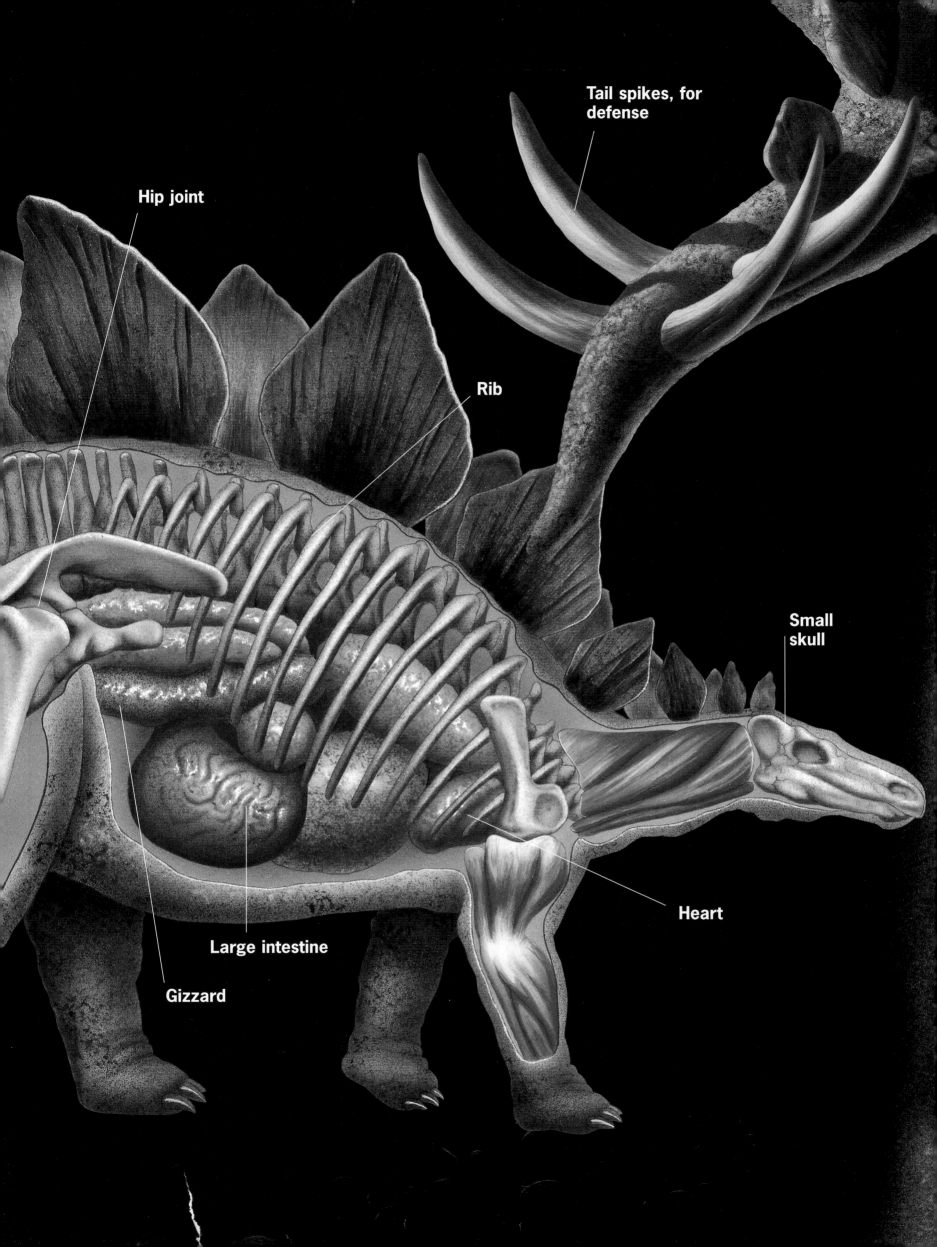

Tail spikes, for defense

Hip joint

Rib

Small skull

Heart

Large intestine

Gizzard

STEGOSAURS

The roughly 15 members of the two known stegosaur families all shared a very special body feature—two long row of staggered bony plates or spines that ran down the center of their backs. They appear to have evolved during the early-to-mid-Jurassic, probably in China, and were most numerous during the late Jurassic. They spread across the world, and fossils have been found in China, Africa, Europe, India, and North America. By the early Cretaceous Period, they had died out everywhere except for India, where they survived until the end of the Cretaceous.

As well as leaves and grass, stegosaurs probably fed on fruit. Here, a stegosaur munches on a cycad fruit. ▼

FOOD AND EATING

All stegosaurs were herbivores. They had a narrow snout with a beak that was probably used to poke among branches and ferns to crop off the choicest pieces of vegetation and fruit. They had sturdy cheek teeth to chew up tough vegetation before they swallowed it.

Examples of cheek ▼ *teeth from three different stegosaurs. All were well-suited to eat foliage.*

Stegosaurus

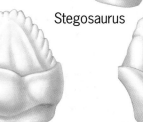

Tuojiangosaurus   Kentrosaurus

THE SKELETON

This *Stegosaurus* skeleton shows the main features of all stegosaurs: the front legs shorter than the back ones; the small narrow head; the large bony plates, or spikes, depending on the species; and the tail spikes.

Bony plates

Narrow, elongated head

Longer hind legs

Shorter front legs

Tail spikes

POSITION OF THE PLATES

Until 1992, when an almost complete *Stegosaurus* skeleton was discovered, scientists were unsure how the plates were distributed along the animals' backs. They now know that they were attached in two staggered rows.

SELF-DEFENSE

Stegosaurs occupied the earth at the same time as some very large, fierce predators, such as *Allosaurus*. They were hefty animals that could not rely on speed or agility to escape, but they were still able to defend themselves. Faced with an attacker, stegosaurs could bellow, rustle their plates, and swipe their lethal tails from side to side.

▲ Kentrosaurus *had six pairs of bony plates on its neck and back, and seven pairs of bony spines to protect its tail.*

▲ *Nearly complete fossils of* Stegosaurus, *like the one above, have helped scientists reconstruct these creatures.*

KENTROSAURUS

This stegosaur lived in East Africa and was much smaller than the *Stegosaurus*. As well as the plates and spikes on its back, *Kentrosaurus* had pair of spines attached at the pelvis that pointed backward.

FUNCTION OF THE PLATES

Over the years, there have been many different theories about what purpose the stegosaurs' plates served. A common theory says that they were used to regulate the animals' body temperature. The plates were covered with flesh and blood, and if the stegosaur stood in the sun, they would grow hot quickly to provide it with energy. They could also be used to cool the animals down, since the plates staggered along the back allowed better access for cool breezes. Where more than one species of stegosaur inhabited the same environment, the variously shaped plates or spines may have been used by the different species to recognize each other. The plates may also have been used in courtship rituals. Most obviously, the large spines and plates were almost certainly used in defense.

TUOJIANGOSAURUS

This stegosaur lived in southern China during the late Jurassic. It takes its name —"Tuo River lizard"—from the river where its well-preserved skeletons have been found. It was about the same size as the *Stegosaurus*, but had cone-shaped plates along its back.

THE CONTINENTS

When the Cretaceous began, the world's landmasses were joined in two super-continents. In the north, Europe, Asia, and North America formed Laurasia. In the south, Africa, South America, Antarctica, Australia, and India formed Gondwana. The two may have been joined at their western end by a land bridge between the Americas. During the Cretaceous, most of the continents split from each other. By the end of the period, they were nearly all separated; Australia and Antarctica were still connected, but India was apart from Asia.

Mid-Cretaceous

Late Cretaceous

▲

At the same time the continents divided, sea levels rose and flooded low-lying areas to form vast shallow seas. These seas made climates wet and warm in most places. Even at the poles, the weather was rarely freezing. The seas divided the continents into smaller landmasses. This meant that animals could not move easily from one place to another, so different dinosaurs evolved in different areas of the world. This would have a profound effect in the late Cretaceous.

THE CRETACEOUS WORLD

The Cretaceous was the third and longest of the periods in the Mesozoic Era, or the "age of dinosaurs." It began about 144 mya and lasted for nearly 80 million years. The Cretaceous is generally divided into early Cretaceous (144 to 85 mya) and late Cretaceous (85 to 66 mya). It was during the Cretaceous that dinosaurs were at their most diverse, and many different types dominated life on earth. It was a time of change for life and for the continents, which separated and collided with each other. At the end of the Cretaceous, there was a sudden mass extinction of many species. All the dinosaurs died out, as did many other animals. Earth became almost an empty planet.

Magnolia is one of the most primitive flowering plants still alive today.

▲

Vast beds of chalk are typical of rocks laid down in the Cretaceous Period. The chalk is made up of billions of shells from tiny sea creatures. The name Cretaceous means "chalky."

FLOWERING PLANTS

At the start of the Cretaceous, plant life was much as it had been for the previous 100 million years. There were large conifer trees, ferns, and a variety of palm-like plants that are now extinct. By the end of the Cretaceous, plants had changed dramatically. Flowering plants took over almost completely. The first flowering plants lived about 140 mya close to the equator in the tropical forests that covered Siberia and southern parts of North America. They were probably woody shrubs, like modern magnolias. They spread slowly until about 115 to 100 mya, when they evolved into a wide array of trees, shrubs, bulbs, herbs, and other forms. Dinosaurs and other animals evolved to eat the new types of food.

Wasps first appeared in the early Cretaceous and have changed little since. ▶

EVOLUTION OF OTHER ANIMALS

Many new animals appeared in the Cretaceous Period. The dinosaurs evolved into many forms, but they were not alone. New types of insects included bees, moths, wasps, butterflies, and ants. Snakes first appeared at this time and, along with crocodiles, were among the few to survive the mass extinction at the end of the Cretaceous. The rapid evolution of new forms of animal life was driven by the changing world. As the climate grew hotter and wetter, animals had to adapt to survive. They also had to cope with the rise of flowering plants, which provided a range of new foods for plant-eating animals. The division of the landmasses into many small continents and large islands allowed different animals to evolve in different areas, then to spread when the shallow seas occasionally retreated.

▲ Fossil of a short-tailed pterosaur. Long-tailed pterosaurs did not survive the transition from the Jurassic to the Cretaceous.

FLYING REPTILES AND BIRDS

The early Cretaceous skies were dominated by pterodactyls. These flying reptiles had long wings formed of a flap of skin stretched over a huge, extended finger. Unlike earlier flying reptiles, pterodactyls had a very small tail or no tail at all. Some grew to enormous size, with wingspans of over 39 feet (12 m). As pterodactyls grew larger, smaller birds took over the lifestyles left vacant. By the end of the Cretaceous, birds had become the dominant flying animals.

▲ Fossils of clams with ridged shells, very similar to those in the oceans today.

Nyctosaurus. *a typical pterodactyl, had long, narrow wings up to 10 feet (3 m) across and a short body with no tail.* ▶

▶ Presbyornis *lived at the very end of the Cretaceous and resembled a long-legged duck. It ate plants in shallow freshwater lakes.*

MARINE LIFE

The warm, shallow seas were rich in animal life of all kinds. Bivalve shellfish, such as clams, were especially common, and new animals evolved to prey on them. Crabs used claws to crack them open, starfish developed muscular arms to pull the shells open, and snails evolved with a drill-like tooth to punch holes in the shells. Marine reptiles also flourished. Long-necked plesiosaurs and short-necked pliosaurs reached very large sizes. There were, however, long periods when life at sea declined sharply. This occurred when ocean currents stopped and oxygen levels fell, which stifled life in many areas.

PLACENTAL MAMMALS AND MARSUPIALS

The first mammals evolved in the later Triassic Period, about 210 mya. For millions of years after, mammals remained rare and small. The only mammal fossils found by scientists in Jurassic and early Cretaceous rocks are a few teeth and pieces of bone. From about 110 mya on, however, the number and variety of mammals increased dramatically. About 100 mya, the marsupials —mammals that keep their young in pouches— first appeared.

◀ Alphadon *an early mammal from the late Cretaceous.*

▲ Dromaeosaurus *was a hunting dinosaur that lived in Asia and North America during the Cretaceous. Dinosaurs from this group had large, curved claws on their hind feet, which were used to slash at prey.*

Centrosaurus *belonged to the ceratopsian group. These dinosaurs had long horns on their faces and frills of bone on the backs of their heads.* ◀

▲ Avimimus *belonged to a group of Asian dinosaurs that could run very fast. Like other fast-running dinosaurs, it probably had a covering of feathers.*

New Sea Predators

New Cretaceous predators, the seagoing flippered lizards known as mosasaurs (such as the *Plotosaurus* and the *Mosasaurus* below), grew to 33 feet (10 m) long. The large tail fins helped power them through the water in search of the fish they ate. They used their good vision and highly evolved teeth to catch and eat everything in their path—including each other.

▶ *This reconstruction of the Hoffman mosasaur shows the long, snakelike body and tail that was typical of mosasaurs. It may have grown to be about 30 feet (9 m) long. The fossil skull of this creature is shown below left.*

In 1786, workmen quarrying chalk near the Dutch town of Maastricht found a set of massive fossilized jaws with ferociously sharp teeth. The fossils were bought by a local scientist named Hoffman, and named after him. Some scientists thought the jaws were from a whale; others said they were from a crocodile. In 1800, scientists learned they belonged to a gigantic lizard, and the fossil was named mosasaur, which means "lizard from Maas". Later fossils showed that the jaws belonged to a swimming lizard, a successful marine predator from the Cretaceous seas. Since then, many similar mosasaur fossils have been found around the world.

The jaws were more than 3 feet (1 m) long, but since then, longer jaws have been found.

The jaws of the mosasaur found at Maastricht were broken in the process of fossilization.

▶ *Elasmosaurus was one of the most extraordinary sea reptiles of all time. Its neck was about 26 feet (8 m) long, much longer than the rest of the body and tail. It used its neck to dart out and snap up fish.*

ARCHELON TURTLE

This gigantic turtle lived in the shallow seas that covered much of North America in the late Cretaceous. It grew to almost 13 feet (4 m) in length and was one of the largest turtles that ever lived. The shell was a leathery skin stretched over bony plates. The front flippers were much larger than the rear, and probably provided most of the power for swimming. The rear flippers may have been used to steer. Its jaws were very weak, so *Archelon* may have fed on jellyfish, which swarmed in large numbers. *Archelon* was so huge that few predators dared to attack it.

PLESIOSAURS

These sea reptiles swam with four large paddles. They evolved during the Jurassic, but when the fishlike ichthyosaurs died in the Cretaceous, the plesiosaurs took over. There were two lines of evolution among plesiosaurs. The first had long necks and small heads and probably ate fish. The second line had short necks and large heads with powerful jaws. They probably hunted other sea reptiles as well as sharks and larger fish.

▲ *Kronosaurus was the largest and most powerful of all the sea reptiles. It grew to be almost 42 feet (13 m) long and had jaws stronger than those of Tyrannosaurus. It probably hunted other sea reptiles.*

LIFE IN THE SEA

As the shallow seas expanded and shrank several times during the Cretaceous Period, life in the seas changed dramatically. Older forms of life vanished and new types appeared. Some later became extinct, but others are still around today.

Champsosaurus looked like a crocodile, but was more closely related to lizards. With its powerful jaws and needle-sharp teeth, the Champsosaurus was a specialized hunter of fish.

TELEOSTS AND NEW SHARKS

Modern sharks evolved from earlier forms at the start of the Cretaceous. The new sharks, or neoselachians, kept the cartilage skeleton of earlier sharks, but the backbone was strengthened with bonelike calcium. Among the bony fish there was a revolution as teleosts, or ray-finned fish, evolved explosively to take over the seas. By the end of the Cretaceous, teleosts were by far the most numerous fish in almost every water habitat.

Modern sharks are very similar to those that cruised the Cretaceous oceans. Unlike earlier sharks, these new sharks had a flexible joint in the jaws that allowed them to open their mouths very wide to bite off large chunks of a victim's flesh.

▲ BONY FISH

The first fish with skeletons of bone appeared about 400 mya. They quickly divided into two main groups: the lobe-finned fish with muscular bases to the fins, and the ray-finned fish with fins that grew directly from the body. The ray-finned fish took over the world in the Cretaceous. The lobe-finned fish almost became extinct. Only the coelocanth survived in deep waters.

FRESHWATER AND SWAMPS

Changes similar to those in the oceans also took place in rivers and swamps. Families of fish that had dominated for more than 100 million years became extinct. In their place, teleost fish flourished and a variety of reptiles specially adapted to hunt these slippery prey appeared. The waters were also home to many species of crocodiles. Unlike most large reptiles, the crocodiles survived the mass extinction at the end of the Cretaceous and continue to live in warm waters to this day.

ON THE SEABED

The bottom of the sea was not always the best place to live. For millions of years, few things could live in the large stretches of seabed starved of oxygen and blanketed in thick, black mud. At other times, the sunlit shallow seas swarmed with life. Cretaceous animals evolved to cope with changing conditions. Bivalve shellfish, such as clams and oysters, were very successful and lived in vast numbers. Some of these grew to be $6\frac{1}{2}$ feet (2 m) across and formed large beds of shells.

Starfish appeared in the Cretaceous and became specialized shellfish hunters. The starfish gripped the two shells in its arms and pulled them apart to eat the animal inside.

Deinosuchus was the largest crocodile that ever lived. It reached about 49 feet (15 m) long and probably hunted larger dinosaurs as they drank at rivers or lakes.

Fighting over Females

Two male *Pachycephalosaurus* charge at each other during a head-butting fight over females. These dinosaurs had massively thick skull bones, which were used in these bone-crunching contests. The male that could butt hardest won the fight—and was able to pair off with a female.

The Australian dinosaur Muttaburrasaurus, had a bulging nose. If the dinosaur blew hard into skin stretched over the nose bones, it would create a loud, booming call. ▼

COURTSHIP AND MATING

All animals need to mate in order to produce young and keep the species going in future generations. Each species has its own way to attract or choose a mate. Some species use rituals or signals. Dinosaurs and other animals would probably have had courtship rituals just as complicated as those of modern animals.

CALLING

Many animals, particularly those that live in forests, call to each other. The sounds travel for long distances so that animals know others are present even when they cannot see them. This can be important in courtship. A female can give a special call to let any nearby males know that she is ready to mate. Some dinosaurs had special cavities and skin pouches that would have helped amplify their calls. They may have used these to call through the forests as part of their courtship rituals.

CONTINUING THE SPECIES

If a species is to survive, adults must mate and produce young. It is not clear how dinosaurs mated, but scientists believe their habits were similar to those of modern reptiles or birds.

The Iberomesornis lived in Spain in the early Cretaceous. Unlike later birds, it had teeth like its dinosaur ancestors. It probably lived in dense forests, and so may have had brightly colored plumage, especially during nesting season.

USING COLOR AND SIGNALS

One of the most common ways for an animal to attract a mate is to display bright colors or exhibit part of its body to the prospective partner. Many modern reptiles have flaps of skin that can be raised to show off to a mate. These flaps are often brightly colored to make them more visible. Dinosaurs probably also had bright patches of skin for this purpose. Some scientists believe a group of fast-running carnivorous dinosaurs evolved special scales on their skins, which may have been erected to create distinctive displays.

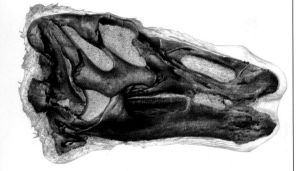

The fossil of Edmontosaurus shows that it had a flap of skin over its nose and snout that could be inflated. This probably made its call louder (see above), but may also have been for display. ▼

▲ Triceratops had a large frill of bone at the rear of its skull. Normally, this would have lain flat along its back, but if the head nodded forward, the frill stood up like the tail of a peacock. It may have been a display to attract a mate.

◄ Many dinosaurs of the hadrosaur group had large crests of bone on top of their skulls. If they were covered in brightly colored skin, these crests would have been effective displays. Hadrosaurs may have been able to change the colors of these crests, as some modern lizards change their skin color.

Spinosaurus, *a hunter from Africa, was 39 feet (12 m) long. On its back it had a large sail of skin* ▶ *supported by thin bone rods that stuck out from its spine. This may have been a brightly colored display to make it look larger to frighten off rival males.*

WARDING OFF RIVALS

As well as attracting mates, animals need to fend off rivals. Some displays could have been used to frighten away a rival male, rather than to attract a female. A male dinosaur would have taken a stand on the area of ground chosen for breeding and displayed or called to females. If another male appeared, the display would change suddenly. The male would roar or hiss to show it was angry. Then it would try to show that it was a large, powerful beast that should be left alone.

◀ *If displays did not make one of the males back down, the rivals might engage in a ritualized conflict. This let the animals discover which was stronger without starting a real fight that could lead to serious injury. These Pteranodons knock their beaks together in a ritual fight.*

Male Ornithocheirus *called loudly to females and flashed their brightly colored bills. If their wings were damaged in fights for territory, they may have been unable to fly, and might have been killed by carnivorous dinosaurs.* ▼

FIGHTING FOR TERRITORY AND FEMALES

Mating and courtship is not always easy, and modern animals often resort to aggression in order to breed. Scientists believe that some prehistoric animals behaved in the same way. *Pteranodons* most likely used their beaks and 6-foot-long (1.8 m) heads to claim territory and attract females. Opponents would have smacked beaks together to try to knock their rival off balance. When one of the *pteranodons* retreated, it meant he had lost. Just as male deer fight with their antlers, the horned dinosaurs used their frills and horns. They may have locked horns and wrestled until the weaker of the two backed off.

Pentaceratops *males displayed their large neck frills as they prepared to fight. If this did not produce a winner, they would fight with their long, sharp horns.* ▼

THE MALE PTEROSAUR SACRIFICE

Many paleontologists believe that pterosaurs had very specific breeding sites. Like some modern animals, pterosaurs probably mated only once a year, so it was very important that they were successful. The males arrived at the chosen territory first and staked out a position. Each male needed enough room to show off its wingspan. Space was limited, so aggression and competition were fierce. Females arrived later, surveyed the rows of males, and chose a partner based on the size of the wings and the beak crests. Fights often broke out during the courtship displays, which lasted for a few days. Many males died from heat exhaustion or from wounds received in fights.

◀ *The* Pteranodon *was a flying pterodactyl with a large crest of bone at the rear of its skull. This crest may have been brightly colored or may have had a flap of skin or hair that could be erected to frighten rival males.*

Nesting Colonies of the Giants

Hadrosaurs, or duck-billed dinosaurs, lived in large herds during the Cretaceous Period. In breeding season, all the females laid their eggs at the same time to form a vast colony. Too heavy to sit on their eggs, the giant mothers-to-be probably covered their nests with vegetation, and then tended their young once they had hatched. These baby dinosaurs have just emerged from their hard-shelled eggs to take their first look at the world.

BURIED TREASURE

Fossilized dinosaur eggs have been found at about 200 sites, but there are probably many still hidden. They look just like stones, and may lie hidden for many more years.

This clutch of eggs was laid by a Therizinosaurus between 110 and 65 mya. ▼

This fossil shows a mother Oviraptor on top of her eggs. She died 80 mya, as she protected them from a storm or flood. This suggests that dinosaurs looked after their young. ▼

eggs

arm

claw

foot

Some of these hadrosaur eggs are hatching. Dinosaurs laid many eggs to improve the chances that young dinosaurs would live to become adults. ▼

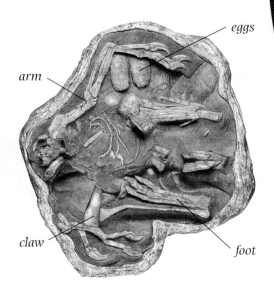

MOTHERS AND EGGS

What was a dinosaur mother like—frightening and fierce or nurturing and gentle? Discoveries of fossilized eggs, baby dinosaurs, nests, and even embryos still inside their eggs have revealed a lot about how dinosaurs nested and how they raised their babies. It is even possible to find out whether they were good parents.

◄ *This fossil shows a dinosaur baby coming out of its egg.*

▲ *This model shows what a Therizinosaurus embryo might have looked like. It seems to be fast asleep but rather cramped in its cozy egg.*

SMALL BEGINNINGS

Some dinosaur eggs were as big as 18 inches (46 cm), but many were small enough to be held in the palm of a human hand. A small egg did not mean the dinosaur would also be small. Many huge dinosaurs hatched fromsmall eggs, just as big oak trees grow from tiny acorn seeds.

▶ *This model shows an embryo in its egg, with blood vessels attached to the yolk, and the umbilical cord attached to the dinosaur's stomach.*

LIVING IN A SHELL

Dinosaurs laid hard-shelled eggs just as birds do today. Eggs had a yolk that held food for the growing embryo (the name for a baby before it is born), and blood vessels that brought food to the embryo. These blood vessels joined in a clump to form a placenta. This led to a tube called an umbilical cord that carried food to the baby's stomach.

▼ Two Maiasaura *mothers look after their young. Some of the babies have started to hatch, and both mothers watch out for Oviraptors (the name means "egg thief") that might want to steal and eat the unhatched eggs. Like many dinosaurs that were too heavy to sit on top of their eggs, this* Maiasaura *(below right) has built a nest out of earth, with high sides to support her body so she does not crush the eggs.*

The name *Maiasaura* means "good mother," and was given to a species of duck-billed dinosaur known to have looked after its young. They built nests, often along riverbanks, and watched their offspring very carefully. Many dinosaurs covered their eggs with plant leaves that gave off heat as they rotted. This would have kept the eggs warm—and very smelly! Many mother dinosaurs returned to the same place each year to breed, and they stayed in large groups and built their nests close together. They stayed in groups to make it harder for predators to steal their eggs. This helped more baby *Maiasaura* to survive. The young stayed in the nest after hatching, and the adult dinosaurs brought them food until they were bigger and better able to look after themselves.

THERMOMETER BEAKS

For an embryo to develop and grow properly inside an egg, it must be kept at exactly the right temperature. If it gets too cold, the baby cannot develop, and if it becomes too hot, it will die. All dinosaur eggs were porous, which means they let air and heat in and out, but it was still difficult to maintain the right temperature. Some dinosaurs developed a clever way of looking after their eggs. They poked their sensitive beaks inside the nest to tell if it was at the right temperature.

▼ *This* Leaellynasaura *mother has covered her eggs with a pile of leaves. She tests the temperature of the nest with her beak.*

Agile Killers

Packs of lethal *Deinonychus* scoured the Cretaceous countryside in search of prey. Although quite small—a fully grown animal was about 10 feet (3 m) long and weighed 130 pounds (60 kg) —these hunters would have terrified even the largest herbivores. Armed with a deadly swiveling toe claw (*Deinonychus* means "terrible claw") and powerful jaws with saw-edged teeth to tear their victims' flesh, they hunted in packs, much as wolves do today. Like these *Deinonychus* that have attacked a huge *Triceratops*, they were able to bring down prey several times larger than themselves.

CLAWS AND JAWS

The most important weapons for hunting are powerful jaws full of sharp teeth for biting, and large, strong claws able to rip through flesh or grasp at prey.

TERRIBLE BITE

Tyrannosaurus's jaws were so powerful, and the long, curved teeth so sharp, they could bite right into bone. The neck was strong, and smaller prey could be picked up and shaken to death.

◀ *The longest dinosaur tooth ever found (left), 16 inches (40 cm), is perfectly made to tear flesh. This one belonged to a Gigantosaurus, which could mortally wound prey with a single bite.*

CARNIVORES

The most terrible and feared of all the dinosaurs, meat-eaters ruled the earth during the Cretaceous Period. Some grew incredibly big in order to hunt giant herbivores. Others were scavengers that used their sense of smell to find corpses. Many hunted in packs to overcome their prey. Each species had its own way to kill victims. They often used fearsome claws and razor-sharp teeth. Although many ate large herbivores, other carnivores fed on small mammals or fish.

This corpse is enough to feed a Tyrannosaurus for several days. ▶

POWERFUL CLAWS

Many carnivores had large claws that could swing down to cut a victim to shreds, or to grip smaller prey. The biggest claws ever found belonged to a *Megaraptor*, and were used to slash prey into pieces.

WELL-DESIGNED

Tyrannosaurus evolved into an awesome killing machine. The tail could not balance the weight of the huge head, so the arms were small and light but ended in two sharp claws.

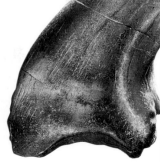

Measuring 11 inches (27 cm), this Megaraptor toe-claw (right, and shown to scale above) is like a huge curved knife.

THE SKILL OF THE CHASE

Carnivorous dinosaurs had different ways to find food. Large carnivores such as *Gigantosaurus* took a big bite, then waited for the victim to bleed to death. Others used their powerful hind legs to chase prey, or attacked the old or weak animals in a herd. Smaller species often hunted in packs, and used teamwork to attack from all sides. Some carnivores scavenged for corpses more than they hunted. This was less dangerous and saved energy. They would have needed a very good sense of smell to find the carrion (dead bodies), and had to be fierce enough to frighten off any others who might want to share the feast.

FOOD CHAIN
Herbivores had to eat vast quantities of vegetation, which gives little energy, to survive, but many carnivores could survive for several days on the corpse of a herbivore, since meat gives more energy. A few huge carnivores ate other smaller meat-eaters as well as herbivores.

large carnivores

carnivores

herbivores

vegetation

SLIPPERY CATCH
Baryonyx fed on fish. They could grab them from the water with long, narrow, snapping jaws that were similar to a crocodile's, and held on to their slippery catch with hooked thumb claws and a vicelike grip. The spiny sail on their backs acted as a fin to help them move quickly in the water, where they waited for fish to swim by.

SWOOPING FROM THE SKY
Carnivores hunted from the skies as well as on land. Birdlike pterosaurs had an excellent view from the sky, and could swoop down to snatch fish from lakes and seas with their long beaks, or find carrion washed ashore to eat. This *Tapejara* had a 17-foot (5 m) wingspan, but unlike other pterosaurs that could glide for hundreds of miles, it flew slowly because the brightly colored crest on its beak was three times as big as its head. This made it difficult not to be blown off balance by the wind. The crest was probably used to attract females during mating season.

▶ *Triceratops might have flashed warning colors on the frill or bony crest on their heads to try to intimidate a predator.*

This unlucky Parasaurolophus has become dinner, but not before hooting to warn its herd of the presence of a predator. ▼

FAST AND BRIGHT
The biggest dinosaurs were not always the most dangerous. Intelligence and speed could be just as deadly. *Velociraptors,* like this one (right), could run at over 31 miles (51 km) an hour, and may have been able to communicate with each other as they hunted in packs.

Velociraptors had narrow jaws like a crocodile's, and razor-sharp toe-claws that could swing forward to ◀ *puncture skin.*

Plates of bony studs

Tail club made up of two clumps of bony tissue

Heavily reinforced skull about 3 feet (1 m) long. There was not much room left for the brain.

Beak

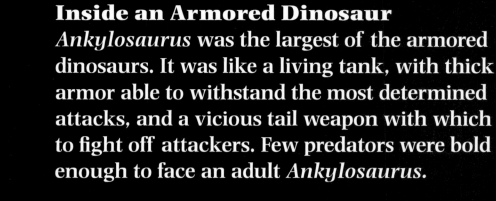

Inside an Armored Dinosaur

Ankylosaurus was the largest of the armored dinosaurs. It was like a living tank, with thick armor able to withstand the most determined attacks, and a vicious tail weapon with which to fight off attackers. Few predators were bold enough to face an adult *Ankylosaurus*.

Wide hips, 10 feet (3 m), to help swing its tail

Large intestine to digest huge quantities of plant material

Flexible tail

Powerful leg muscles to move the heavy body, which weighs up to 7 tons

Soft underbelly

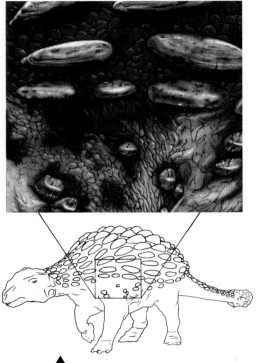

A fossilized section of Ankylosaurus hide. The skin is studded with plates of bone of various sizes, but all are thick enough to stop the claws of a predator.

WHAT'S IN A NAME?

The two families of armored dinosaurs are closely related to each other and have names that describe their armor. The nodosaurids were named for the nodules of bone on their armored skin. These nodules fit closely together to form an inflexible sheet. The name *ankylosaur* means "joined together reptile," and refers to the bands of solid bone that ran side to side across the back of this dinosaur. The armor of the ankylosaurs was flexible, and allowed them to move more easily.

Polacanthus was a nodosaurid that lived in Europe about 120 mya. As well as armor nodules, it had long spikes that it ▶ probably used to fend off predators. There were no spines in the hip area, where the armor was thickest.

Armored dinosaurs have been ▶ found mainly on the northern continents. The older nodosaurid family has been found in Europe and North America, but the later ankylosaurids have been found in western North America and eastern Asia. The ankylosaurids probably evolved from nodosaurids that lived in North America about 110 mya.

● Ankylosaurids
● Nodosaurids

ARMORED DINOSAURS

The armored dinosaurs appeared in Europe at the very start of the early Cretaceous, and later spread to North America and parts of Asia. They were medium-sized dinosaurs, about 10 to 26 feet (3–8 m) in length, but were massively built with heavy bodies and solid bone armor. They walked on all four legs and ate plants. Scientists have found relatively few fossils of these dinosaurs. This may mean that there were not many of them, or that they lived in areas where fossils do not often form, such as mountains.

▶ Nodosaurus lived in North America about 95 mya. The tough bone armor ran from the top of its head, along its back, to the tip of its tail.

THE NODOSAURIDS

The nodosaurids were the more primitive armored dinosaurs. They walked on all fours and were protected by armor plates and spikes. The skulls were made of thick bones, and had small, simple teeth and a pointed beak at the front of the jaws. They probably ate low-lying vegetation that did not need to be chewed much.

Pinacosaurus *was about 16 feet (5 m) long, but was much more slender than most other armored dinosaurs. It lived in North America about 80 mya. Like other armored* ▶ *dinosaurs, it had small, weak teeth. Some scientists think it ate soft fruits rather than tough leaves or stalks.*

ARMORED PLATING

Nodosaurids and ankylosaurids used their armor to defend themselves against hunting dinosaurs. At the time the armored dinosaurs lived, hunters included such powerful giants as *Tyrannosaurus* and *Albertosaurus.* Many dinosaurs had bony studs through the skin, but in the armored dinosaurs, these covered almost the entire body surface. The back of the neck, body, and tail were encased in solid sheets of bone from which ridges, spikes, and knobs stuck out. The skulls were especially well protected. The creatures had thick skull bones, as well as great slabs of bone grown from the skin to cover the head. In some species, the eyes and nostrils were covered with armor, too.

THE ANKYLOSAURIDS

The more advanced ankylosaurs evolved about 110 mya in Asia or North America, but never spread to Europe. Their armor was more flexible and complete than that of the nodosaurids—even the eyelids had a bone covering. At the end of their muscular tails, the ankylosaurs had a large lump of solid bone that weighed many pounds. It could swing from side to side as a weapon to fight off attackers. A blow from the club would have been able to cripple or even kill a predator such as *Tyrannosaurus.*

▶ *One of the best known armored dinosaurs was* Euoplocephalus, *which means "true plated head." Scientists have found several skeletons and many examples of the armor of this massive creature. As well as the usual ankylosaur armor, this dinosaur had spikes on its shoulders and the back of its head, and smaller spines on its back.*

▶ *Three views of an* Ankylosaurus *tail.*

▲ *To face a large attacker, nodosaurids would have crouched close to the ground and gripped the earth with their claws. Only their heavily armored upper surfaces would have been exposed. The softer underbelly of the* Hylaeosaurus *was safe from injury, pressed to the ground.*

DEFENSIVE STRATEGIES

The armored dinosaurs would have relied on their armor for defense, but that does not mean they did not have an active strategy for repelling attacks. All armored dinosaurs were strong, mobile creatures that were probably able to break into a lumbering trot. When faced with a small or medium-sized attacker, they would probably lower their armored heads and charge, hoping to bulldoze the enemy to the ground. A charging 4-ton dinosaur with solid bone armor and sharp spikes would have been a fearsome sight.

Against larger predators, such as the *Tyrannosaurus,* this tactic might not have been successful since the hunter itself had fearsome weapons.

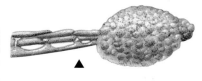
▲ *Profile and view from above of* Euoplocephalus *tail.*

▶ *The ankylosaurids used their tail club as a weapon against predators. They would probably have turned their backs to the danger and lashed their tails from side to side. Few attackers would have risked the crippling blows such a weapon could deliver.*

▶ *Fossils of two different ankylosaurid tail clubs have been found by paleontologists.*

THE TAIL CLUB

Few animals in earth's history have had a weapon like the tail club of the ankylosaurids. It was made up of bone plates in the skin, which were massively enlarged and fused to the last few bones of the tail. In most species, these formed two distinct knobs of bone, one on either side of the tail. A few species had large spikes that grew out of the tail sides to increase the destructive power of the weapon. Very thick tendons ran from the tail club to the base of the tail, where they linked to powerful muscles attached to the hips. These muscles were able to swing the club with great force from side to side, but not up and down. Clearly, the weapon was used to sweep a few feet above the ground to strike the legs of an attacker.

The Giant of Flying Reptiles
The largest flying animal of all time was the *Quetzalcoatlus*, which soared across North American skies at the very end of the Cretaceous Period. With a wingspan of about 39 feet (12 m) and a weight of around 189 pounds (86 kg), this true giant of the air was able to soar for hours on the warm air currents that rose from the hot, humid landscape below.

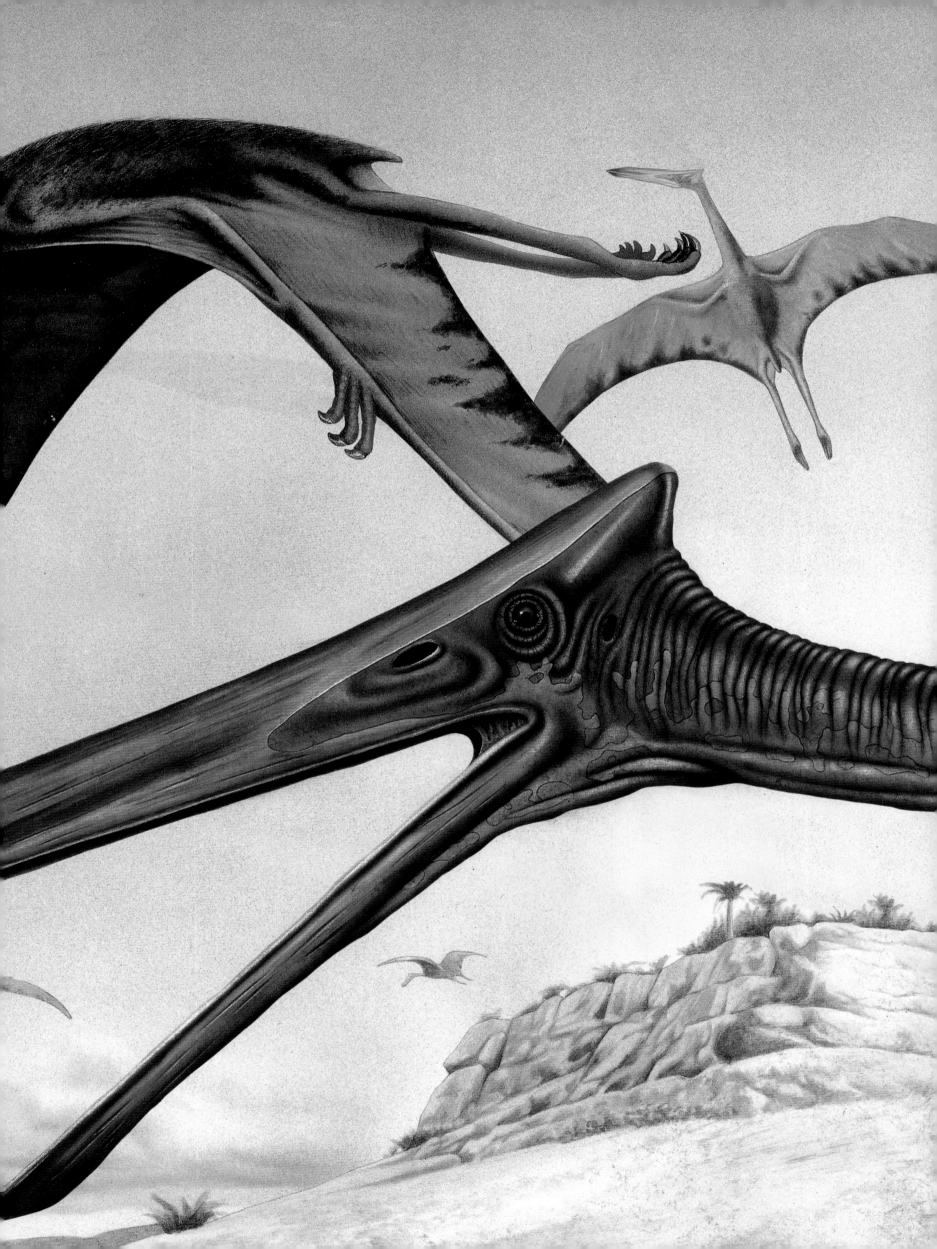

LIFE IN THE AIR

As the world changed during the Cretaceous, the range and types of flying animals adapted. The flying reptiles, the pterosaurs, were no longer the only large flying creatures. Birds became increasingly numerous and important. The long-tailed pterosaurs died out, which left only the short-tailed pterosaurs, or pterodactyls. These grew increasingly large over time, until they became true giants. At the end of the Cretaceous, everything changed as the pterosaurs became extinct.

▲

Bees appeared for the first time in the Cretaceous. It is thought they may have evolved to take advantage of the new food source available from the nectar and pollen of flowering plants, also new in the Cretaceous.

▶

The fish-eating Hesperornis *lacked muscles strong enough for flight, and probably spent all its life in the sea, diving for fish and other marine animals.*

PHOBETOR

Th̶... ...retaceous pterosaur with a ...ut 5 feet (2 m). It had long, pointed jaws that had teeth only in the rear, and long, pointed wings that let it soar on rising air currents. *Phobetor*'s most obvious feature, however, was the crests on its skull. A long spike grew back from behind the eyes, and a thin ridge of bone ran down the center of the skull from the eye to halfway along the jaws. It is thought that *Phobetor* lived near inland lakes and rivers, where it used its long jaws to probe the mud for worms and shellfish.

WIDE RANGE OF SPECIES

There may have been a greater range of flying animals in the Cretaceous than at any other time in earth's history. The reptilian pterosaurs that had first flown in the Triassic were still numerous, but birds also advanced quickly. A bird named *Concornis* from early Cretaceous Spain had strong muscles and was clearly capable of skilled flight. There were also many types of flying insects such as butterflies, moths, bees, and wasps, which all appeared for the first time. There may even have been a few small mammals able to glide from tree to tree, which began the evolutionary journey that would produce bats.

▶

Tropeognathus *had a wingspan of about 20 feet (6 m). The wings were very thin, which helped* Tropeognathus *ride the air currents that blew over the tropical oceans where it fished for food.*

▶

Ichthyornis *resembled a modern tern or gull, with a larger head and teeth in its jaws. It was a strong flier and probably cruised long distances in search of marine prey.*

TROPEOGNATHUS

The name *Tropeognathus* means "ship's keel jaw," and refers to the bulges of bone at the tips of the jaws. These were large, but very flat and narrow. It is thought that they helped the creature keep its head steady as it swept its jaws through the surface waters of the shallow seas that covered what is now South America. It is likely the animal flew low over the water with its jaws dipped into the waves ready to snap up any fish or creature they touched. The sharp, interlocking teeth would have held the slippery fish firmly until the *Tropeognathus* had time to eat it.

👁

The Cretaceous World 68 • Courtship and Mating 76 • The Giant of Flying Reptiles 90

ANHANGUERA

The name of this early Cretaceous pterosaur means "the old devil" in the language of the Tupi tribe in the area of Brazil where the fossils were found. The hips and leg bones of this pterosaur show that it was unable to walk on its hind legs like modern birds and some other flying reptiles. On land, it probably shuffled along on all fours with its wings tucked back over its body. The unusual feature of this creature is the skull, which was almost as long as the body. This would have made it unstable in flight if the skull bones had not been paper-thin and very light.

▲
The Anhanguera had a short crest of bone that rose from the upper jaw and stuck out from under the lower jaw. This helped keep the jaws steady when they plunged into the water to snap up fish as the pterosaur flew low above the waves.

PTERODAUSTRO

This pterosaur lived in South America about 130 mya, at the start of the Cretaceous Period. It was much smaller than most later flying reptiles, with a wingspan of 4 feet (1.5 m). The *Pterodaustro* had long, thin, slightly flexible teeth that stuck up from the lower jaw. The thousand or so teeth formed a highly effective sieve. It is likely the *Pterodaustro* waded through shallow lakes, and dipped its jaws into the water to filter out tiny shrimps and other creatures. It then licked these up and swallowed.

▶
The Ornithodesmus *is so unlike other pterosaurs that it has been placed in a family of its own.*

ORNITHODESMUS

The wings and body of this fairly large pterosaur are typical of Cretaceous flying reptiles. The wings were long and narrow, and the body was short and squat with a very small tail. The head, however, was unique. Most pterosaurs had pointed jaws, but those of *Ornithodesmus* were wide and ended in a rounded snout like the bill of a modern duck. Unlike a duck, however, this creature had a large number of short, needle-sharp teeth at the front of its jaws. It probably ate fish from the inland lakes and marshes of western Europe where it lived.

◀ *The* Pterodaustro *had bristlelike teeth used to trap fish in shallow waters.*

NESTING

The nesting habits of Cretaceous birds and pterosaurs are a mystery, largely because no fossilized nests or eggs have been found. It is likely, however, that the birds would have nested the way modern birds do. The flightless *Hesperornis* could only walk, so it must have built its nest close to the shore. It is likely that the bird would have chosen mudflats or sandbanks, where land predators could not reach the vulnerable eggs. Pterosaurs, such as the late Cretaceous giant *Pteranodon*, were able to fly, and probably laid their eggs high on cliffs, where they would also have been safe from hunters. It is unclear if pterosaurs incubated the eggs themselves, or if they left them exposed to the sun to allow the warm Cretaceous air to hatch the young. What is known is that very young pterosaurs were unable to fly, so it is certain that the parents would have fed the young, perhaps with half-chewed fish or other easily digested foods that they stored in their beaks.

The Golden Age of Dinosaurs

The late Cretaceous Period saw an explosive growth in the number and variety of dinosaurs and other animals. The dramatic increase in flowering plants, which could produce more plant food than earlier plants, seems to have caused this sudden increase in diversity. Nothing indicated that the existing situation would be suddenly shattered by a mass extinction that would wipe out most living things on earth.

The Oviraptor had a strangely curved beak with a sharp bone spike halfway along the jaws. It probably used the beak to pick up eggs, then cracked them open with the spikes. ◄

Protoceratops (right and below) was one of the first ceratopids. Its skull had the parrot beak of all later dinosaurs in this group. It also has another feature of later ceratopids: a bone frill at the rear of the skull. ▶

HEADS AND SKULLS

The late Cretaceous saw a great diversity of dinosaur species and families. Entirely new types of creatures evolved, then divided into a number of similar species as evolution continued to take place. This period saw some of the most amazing crests, horns, and other head growths that any animals have ever boasted.

BEAKS AND TEETH

Most animals use their mouths and teeth as tools to obtain food. Because of this, scientists study the mouths and teeth of dinosaurs and other extinct animals to find out what foods they ate. A creature with long, sharp teeth may have been a meat-eater, while one with short, blunt teeth probably ate plants. Sometimes, however, the teeth or mouths are so unusual that scientists are not sure what the creature ate. Some teeth may be so specialized that their purpose is a mystery.

Hadrosaurs, such as Anatosaurus, had groups of hundreds of teeth packed into the sides of their jaws, but no teeth towards the front of the mouth (see above). It is thought they nipped pine needles with their beak, then ground the needles to a mushy paste with their side teeth. ▼

HORNED FACES

About 90 mya, a new group of dinosaurs evolved. These creatures had short, narrow beaks shaped like those of a modern parrot, but with strong teeth in the rear of the jaws. These dinosaurs evolved rapidly to become the ceratopids. Soon, large herds of them dominated the land. It is thought that their success came from their beak, which help them feed efficiently on some type of plant that was very plentiful at the time, although scientists are unsure which plant it was.

◄ *Parasaurolophus had a crest that curved backward. This crest was hollow, but may have been brightly colored and used as a signal.*

Lambeosaurus had a big, domed crest that held large air passages. It could have produced loud noises that would have been heard from a great distance. ▶

CRESTS

The hadrosaurs had bone crests on the tops of their skulls. The crests were often hollow, but some were made of solid bone. The purpose of these crests has been explained in a number of ways. Some people thought they were a way to store air when the creature dived underwater. Others said the crests gave the animals a superb sense of smell. Some thought they were used to push tree branches out of the way as the dinosaurs fed. Today, it is believed the hollow crests were used to produce loud sounds. The solid crests were probably brightly colored and used in ritual displays.

FRILLY DINOSAURS

As the ceratopid dinosaurs became more numerous, they evolved large frills of bone that grew from the back of the skull and were often as large as the rest of the head. The origin of these frills may have been bony knobs and ridges to which the animal's powerful jaw muscles were attached. The success of the ceratopids came from their pointed jaws, which had strong muscles to work them. It is thought that as the knobs and ridges on the back of the skull grew, they became linked to mating behavior. Females preferred males with larger bone ridges, perhaps because this showed they had strong muscles and were better feeders. In time, this preference meant the bone ridges grew much larger and became display devices with which ceratopids signaled to each other and resolved disputes over territory or mates. Over thousands of generations, this produced some quite extraordinary head crests. As the crests grew in size, the ceratopids also evolved large horns. These were used as weapons against predators, but may also have been used as a way to communicate with others.

Styracosaurus *had only a short frill of bone on its skull. Instead of a large frill, it had sharp spikes that grew backward, and must have been a frightening sight when it shook its head at rivals.* ▶

Torosaurus *had the largest skull of any land animal ever to live. The skull was about 8½ feet (2.6 m) long, as large as a small car. It had a long frill of bone at the back of the skull, a pair of horns that pointed over the eyes, and a shorter third horn on the nose.* ◀

Triceratops *had a short, solid fringe of bone at the back of the skull and three sharp, stout horns that pointed forward. The name of this dinosaur means "three horn face." At about 29.5 feet (9 m) long, it was one of the largest ceratopids.* ▼

The skull of a Pachycephalosaurus *shows the key features of the bone-headed dinosaurs. The snout is covered with sharp bony knobs, and the back of the skull has larger, more rounded knobs. The top of the skull is shaped like a dome, and the skull roof is thickest behind the eyes. The teeth were able to shred tough plant material, such as fern leaves.* ▶

▲ *At about 6½ feet (2 m) long* Stegoceras *was a relatively small bone-headed dinosaur. It lived in upland areas of North America where fossils are rarely formed, which is why so few of them have been found.*

THICK HEADS

When scientists found the fossils of pachycephalosaurs, they realized quickly they had found an entirely new type of dinosaur. The skulls of these animals are topped by enormously thick domes of solid bone, unlike anything seen in any other animal. Fossils of the bodies are rarely found, but they seem to be similar to other small, plant-eating dinosaurs. It is now accepted that the dinosaurs had head-butting contests to decide which was stronger. This may have settled disputes over feeding grounds or mates. The rivals would have stood a few feet apart, then lowered their heads and charged at full speed. Th... together with great force. Th... become stunned or giv...

▶ *When a predator threatened a group of* Chasmosaurus *ceratopids, they huddled together in a tight group. The largest dinosaurs faced the enemy, and waved their crests and horns to frighten it away. Young or sick animals stayed in the rear, where they were safe from attack.*

The Geological Time Scale

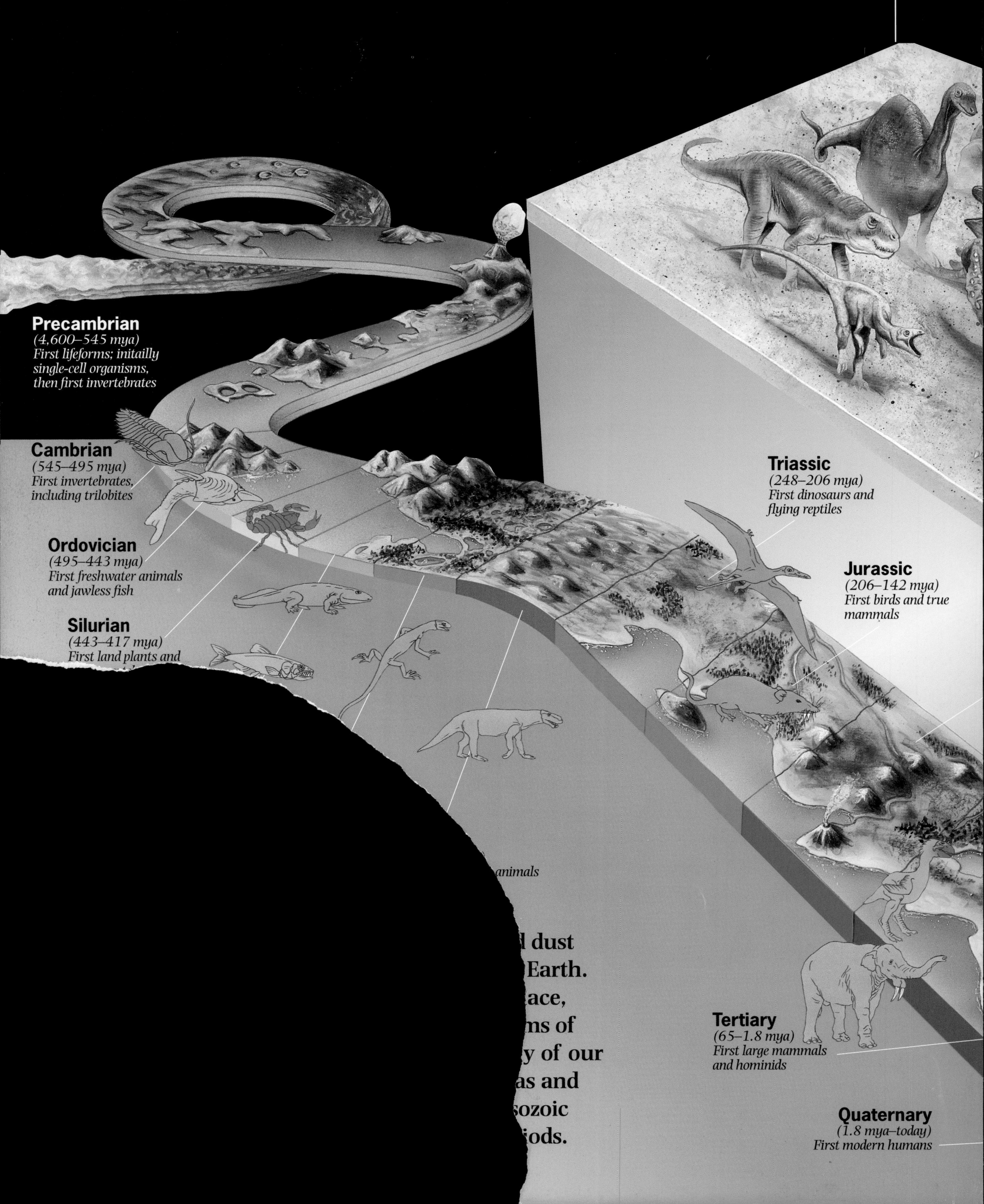

248 mya

Precambrian
(4,600–545 mya)
*First lifeforms; initailly
single-cell organisms,
then first invertebrates*

Cambrian
(545–495 mya)
*First invertebrates,
including trilobites*

Ordovician
(495–443 mya)
*First freshwater animals
and jawless fish*

Silurian
(443–417 mya)
First land plants and

Triassic
(248–206 mya)
*First dinosaurs and
flying reptiles*

Jurassic
(206–142 mya)
*First birds and true
mammals*

animals

*d dust
Earth.
ace,
ns of
y of our
as and
sozoic
ods.*

Tertiary
(65–1.8 mya)
*First large mammals
and hominids*

Quaternary
(1.8 mya–today)
First modern humans

Cretaceous
(142–65 mya)
Frist flowering plants;
End of the dinosaurs

65 mya

The Day the Asteroid Hit
About 65 mya, all the dinosaurs—and many other animals—became extinct. The most popular theory to explain this event is that a gigantic asteroid hit the earth and caused a huge, violent explosion that had devastating effects.

A thin layer of clay between harder rocks marks the boundary between Cretaceous rocks, where dinosaur fossils have been found, and later Tertiary rocks. The Euro coin shows how thin the layer is.

THE METEOR THEORY

For 150 million years or more, dinosaurs were the most dominant form of animal life on earth. Then, about 65 mya, they vanished. Only rocks more than 65 million years old have dinosaur fossils. Many other forms of life also disappeared at the same time. Most scientists believe a dramatic event caused the mass extinction, but they disagree about exactly what happened.

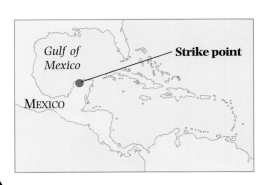

The Chicxulub crater on the coast of Mexico, now buried under 3,000 feet of rock, is where scientists believe the meteor hit.

EVIDENCE FOR THE METEOR THEORY

In 1979, a team from The University of California, Berkeley, led by Walter Alvarez, studied rocks that formed at the change from the Cretaceous to the Tertiary Period (the K/T Boundary). They found the rocks held massive amounts of iridium, a metal that is rare on earth but common in meteorites and asteroids. Alvarez thought a giant meteorite had hit the earth. Since then, K/T rocks from more than 150 sites have been studied. All have had high iridium levels. This suggests that a meteor about 6 miles (10 km) wide struck at a speed of about 12 miles (20 km) a second. The impact would have been as powerful as 100 million H-bombs.

LOCATION OF THE METEOR

Once the meteor theory took hold, scientists began to look for the impact site. If a huge meteor struck the earth, it would leave clear signs. The presence of shocked quartz crystals showed that the collision must have happened on or near land, but signs of giant waves suggested that it was in the sea. Together, this evidence suggests that the meteor hit the coast or shallow seas. A crater about 93–124 miles (150–200 km) across, ringed by mountains, would have been created by the collision. Over the millions of years since the event, the mountains would have eroded down and the crater would have filled with sediments, but the signs could still be seen. In 1991, the remains of such a crater were found off the Yucatán Peninsula in Mexico. The crater was dated to 65 mya. Scientists believed they had found the impact site.

The giant meteor seen at stages as it approached earth. As it came close to impact, it would have begun to burn in the intense heat caused by contact with the atmosphere.

A grain of quartz found in the K/T boundary in Montana. Seen under a microscope, it has lines caused by the pressure shock waves of a meteorite explosion.

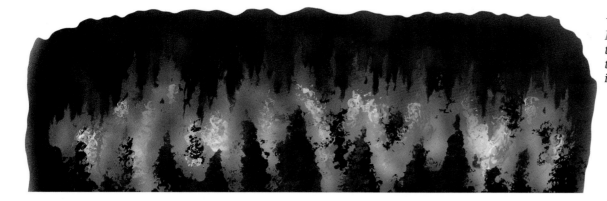

◄ *Molten rock from the exploding meteor caused fires that consumed forests and the life-forms within them. The soot made by these fires has been found in rocks in many areas.*

EFFECTS ON THE ENVIRONMENT

For hundreds of miles around the site of impact, the area would have been totally devastated, and no plants or animals would have survived. Beyond that area, the red-hot debris of molten rock and ash would have caused terrible fires that consumed everything in their reach. Most of North and South America would have been wiped out in this way. Large clouds of ash would have spread through the atmosphere over the rest of the world before they fell as a dense, choking blanket that suffocated life. Finer dust would have stayed in the high atmosphere for up to a year. This would have cut off the sunlight needed for plant life, and caused temperatures to fall dramatically. This would have killed nearly all the plants on earth. Most would have left seeds that could germinate when the sunlight returned, but by that time, the animals that fed on the plants would have died, as would the carnivores that fed on the plant-eating animals.

▲ *A giant wave crashes ashore. The meteor impact would cause a wave up to ⁵/₈ mile (1 km) tall to race across the oceans of the world.*

◄ *The steep drop in temperatures caused when soot blocked out the sun would have led to heavy snowfall in many places.*

A meteorite crater in Arizona. It is over ⁵/₈ mile (1 km) across and was formed by a meteorite that struck earth about 50,000 years ago. A late Cretaceous meteor crater would have been much larger. ▼

DEATH IN THE SEAS

The meteor would have had a tremendous effect on the oceans. It is estimated that 60 percent of all marine life became extinct. Giant waves would have had little effect, but blocked sunlight and disruptions to ocean currents would have been more serious. Most sea reptiles became extinct, although turtles survived, as did ammonite shellfish, many forms of clams and related animals, and many species of fish. Vast numbers of plankton also died out at this time.

Fossils of Edmontosaurus, *one of the dinosaurs that became extinct at the K/T boundary.* ▼

▲ *The* Berycopsis *lived just before the formation of the K/T boundary. Its descendants survived the mass extinction. Up to 40 percent of modern fish descend from this one.*

DEATH ON LAND

Extinctions on land were even more dramatic than those in the sea. All animals over 55 pounds (25 kg) became extinct, along with many smaller species. All the dinosaurs and flying reptiles died, along with large numbers of insects and other animals. Although many mammals did not survive, enough lived to ensure that they recovered. Crocodiles also survived in some numbers, and only certain families of birds were affected. Land plants show almost no sign of extinction at this time. The impact of a meteor would explain most of these changes. A temporary stop of plant growth from blocked sun rays would have killed all the larger animals that relied on regular plant or meat meals. Smaller animals might have been able to hibernate through the worst food shortages and so survive.

Cooling Climate, Volcanoes, and Sea Levels

The dinosaurs may have been wiped out by gradual changes in climate, rather than a single event such as a meteor strike. Scientists who study plant fossils say that by the end of the Cretaceous, tropical plants had given way to species that favor cooler climates. Climate changes may have resulted when huge volcanoes filled the air with smog that blocked out the warming rays of the sun. Changing sea levels also may have affected climate.

WHAT IS A VOLCANO?

A volcano occurs where magma from deep within the earth wells up to the surface and spills out. There are various types of volcanoes, and they have different shapes. Cone volcanoes form where magma solidifies into rock and escapes through a vent at the top. Composite volcanoes tend to have less steep sides than cone volcanoes. Shield volcanoes occur when molten rock flows farther away from the vent before it turns to solid rock and builds a wide slab of new rock. Hawaiian volcanoes form around long cracks in the earth's surface, where magma wells up in long parallel lines and spreads out over wide areas.

Types of volcanoes

Cone volcano

Composite volcano

Shield volcano

Hawaiian volcano

This cross section (below) shows a cone volcano. A reservoir of molten rock, or magma, forms near the surface of the earth and pushes up to spill out as lava that solidifies as it cools. Gradually, a large cone of rock is formed, and may be hundreds of feet high. Underground water near the magma heats to the boiling point. It emerges as geysers and hot springs. ▼

ALTERNATIVE THEORIES

Although the meteor theory is the most popular, it is not the only explanation for the end of the dinosaurs. Some scientists believe that volcanoes, climate changes, or other events led to the extinctions at the end of the Cretaceous. Some think the dinosaurs did not die out suddenly, but over a period of time.

ARGUMENTS AGAINST THE METEOR THEORY

If the meteor theory is correct, the dinosaurs and other animals would have been killed off within one or two years. Fossil records show that the dinosaurs were most numerous about 10 million years before the K/T boundary formed. Their numbers and variety had already begun to fall before they became extinct. There are also signs that the effect of the meteor impact was not as widespread as was first thought. Moths had evolved in the Cretaceous, and they need very clean air to survive. If the world had been covered by a vast cloud of dust, all moths would have died out—but they did not.

THE DECCAN TRAPS AND THEIR EFFECTS

Some scientists believe massive volcanic eruptions may have caused the late Cretaceous extinctions. When the K/T boundary was formed, the world's largest ever volcanic eruptions took place in western India, in an area known as the Deccan Traps. Molten rock and gas flowed out of volcanoes and covered an area half the size of Europe. When the rock solidified, it formed beds over a mile thick. The gas included selenium, which is very toxic to animals as they develop within eggs. This may have caused the extinction of egg-laying animals. The eruptions may also have thrown up vast clouds of dust that partially blocked out the sun and cause climates to cool.

▲ *The Deccan Traps are in western India. The original area covered by lava flows was about 600,000 square miles (1.5 million sq. km).*

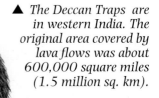

MAMMAL COMPETITION

One early theory about dinosaur extinction suggested that small mammals ate the dinosaur eggs. This would have killed off the egg-laying dinosaurs but allowed the mammals, which give birth to live young, to survive. It is unlikely, however, since the many egg-eating animals in the world today do not drive birds or reptiles to extinction. A newer theory suggests that mammals were better suited to the new climate and new types of plants that emerged at the end of the Cretaceous. Eventually, they may have taken the dinosaurs' place and indirectly caused their extinction.

THE COOLING EFFECT AND CHANGES IN SEA LEVELS

There is clear evidence that climate changed and sea levels fell toward the end of Cretaceous. This would have had a profound impact for life on earth. In the last 10 million years of the Cretaceous, plants that favor a tropical climate with damp, hot weather all year round became much rarer. Plants that prefer a cooler climate with clear seasonal differences grew instead. The fall in sea levels at the same time would have made temperature changes more dramatic, and created an extreme climate with very cold and hot weather. Dinosaurs and animals that had evolved in a more stable climate may have been unable to adapt to the new change.

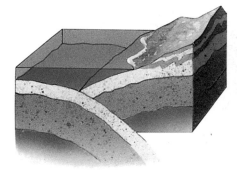

▲ *Continental drift may have changed sea levels and led to a cooler climate. Earth's surface is made up of several layers of rock that float on the semi-liquid core beneath. As these plates move, they either collide or separate. When they collide, one plate slips under the other, which causes earthquakes and builds mountains.*

When plates pull apart, liquid ▲ *rock wells up from below to form new rocks on the surface.*

▲ *A fossil of unhatched dinosaurs. The temperature at which they are stored determines whether eggs of some modern reptiles produce male or female young. If earth's climate cooled, it may have led dinosaurs to produce young of only one sex, which prevented breeding.*

◄ *Some scientists believe that poison killed the dinosaurs.*

THERE ARE MANY OTHER THEORIES

Ever since dinosaur fossils were first discovered, there have been suggestions as to why dinosaurs became extinct. One of the first theories was that the dinosaurs had lived on earth before the flood mentioned in the Book of Genesis in the Bible. Claims were made that, for some reason, Noah did not take the dinosaurs on the ark, and so they had all drowned. Another theory was that a comet collided with earth and the cyanide in the comet's head poisoned the air. This does not explain why some animals died and others survived, however. Some argued that the new types of plants at the end of the Cretaceous were toxic to dinosaurs but not to mammals. There is no real evidence for this idea either. There are many other ideas that have been even stranger than these, but none has convinced most scientists.

▶ *A photograph taken through a telescope. One theory was that a star that exploded close to earth might have blasted the dinosaurs to death. No evidence of such explosion has been found.*

◄ *A cast of a dinosaur brain. In the early twentieth century, some people thought dinosaurs were too stupid to survive, since their brains were so small compared with their bodies.*

1 *Andrewsarchus*
2 *Palaeoryctes*
3 *Coryphodon*
4 *Lophiodon*
5 *Propaleotherium*
6 *Eurotamandua*
7 *Eobasileus*
8 *Hyracotherium*
9 *Hyaenodon*

After the Dinosaurs
The extinction of the dinosaurs left mammals and other animals free to evolve and take the place of the dinosaurs. The rapid evolution of different sorts of animals produced some bizarre life-forms. Eventually, though, post-dinosaur evolution produced the animals we know today.

Tortoises are descendants of turtles that first evolved about 200 mya.

Ferns, such as this stonchlana, are the first to grow after a volcano erupts. After the meteor hit at the K/T boundary, ferns grew in vast numbers across North America.

The sturgeon belongs to the group of bony fish that appeared in the Devonian Period, about 100 million years before the first dinosaurs. Most modern fish belong to a different group, the ray-finned fish.

A Greek frog (Rana greca), that belongs to the most successful modern group of amphibians, the frogs and toads. These creatures evolved before the first dinosaurs, but only became numerous 100 million years later.

THE SURVIVORS

During the Tertiary, mammals began to dominate life on earth. Many other animals also survived the extinctions, however. Several of the oldest life-forms, such as fish and amphibians, continued as did some types of reptiles, such as lizards and snakes. Smaller creatures, such as insects and spiders, also survived and evolved into new species. The first animals to gain from the extinction of the dinosaurs were birds. Within a few million years of the dinosaurs' demise, enormous, flightless birds had evolved. These "terror birds" became extinct only after large, predatory mammals evolved.

Lemurs once lived across most continents. Today, they are found only in Madagascar. More advanced monkeys have driven them to extinction elsewhere.

Insects evolved long before the dinosaurs and lived through the extinction of the dinosaurs and the evolution of the mammals with little change. This giant ant lived in central Europe about 50 mya.

MAMMAL SURVIVORS

At the time the dinosaurs became extinct, few of the modern groups of mammals existed. There were small, shrew-like creatures that scurried at night and ate plants and small animals. There were primitive hedgehogs whose diet was worms and insects. There were also small marsupials and egg-laying monotremes. Several million years passed before larger plant-eaters and hunters of other mammals appeared.

Purgatorius was a mammal that lived to the Tertiary. It was about 4 inches (10 cm) long and probably ate insects. It may have been the first of the primates, a group that includes monkeys, apes, and humans.

HOW DID THE MAMMALS SURVIVE?

If mammals had not survived, life would have been completely different for the past 6 million years, and humans, who are mammals, would never have evolved. At the time of the K/T boundary, mammals were small and very active animals with high body temperatures. Mammals make a great effort to care for their young, and when they are born, they are more developed than reptiles or marsupials. This means that they are more able to cope in times of hardship. Many mammals sleep in burrows, so they may have been safely asleep below ground when the meteor struck. It was probably a combination of these features that helped them survive when so many others died. Whatever the reason for their success, the mammals evolved quickly and dramatically to take advantage of the new world order.

Lepticidium was a small, hopping mammal that lived in Europe about 50 mya. It survived the K/T boundary but became extinct about 25 mya.

AFTER THE DINOSAURS

Earth was suddenly an emptier planet 65 mya. All large animals died out, and only some of the smaller species remained. Gradually, the survivors evolved and adapted to the changed world. Mammals soon became the largest life-forms on earth, but other animals had roles to play as well.

▶ *The Ilingoceros lived in North America about 18 mya and belonged to the Antilocapridae family. Today, only one species from this group survives—the pronghorn.*

▲ *World map – early Tertiary*

EVOLUTION OF LARGER MAMMALS

The largest plant-eaters of the Paleocene were called pantodonts. It was not until about 40 mya, however, that mammals grew to be as large as modern rhinoceroses. The first group to reach this size were the plant-eating *Uintatheres* of North America. Gradually, other types of mammals also grew in size. The largest ever was the *Indricotherium* of China, which grew to about 26 feet (8 m) long. Even this huge beast was only as big as a medium-size dinosaur.

▶ *The hippopotamus evolved only about 12 mya. It is one of the most recent mammals.*

◀ *The anteater* Eurotamandua *lived 40 mya in Europe. It ate insects that it caught with its long, sticky tongue.*

▲ *World map – late Tertiary*

PHYSICAL CHANGES

The world map continued to change during the Tertiary Period. At speeds of less than 1/2 inch (1 cm) a century Australia left Antarctica and moved north, India moved north to hit Asia, Africa moved north toward Europe, and South America moved north to link to North America. The movement of the continents had a profound impact on mammals. Some continents, such as Australia, developed animals entirely different from those elsewhere.

THE FAMILY TREE OF MAMMALS

MAMMALS DIVERSIFY

For several million years, mammals did not change much. Then, about 50 mya, there was an explosion of evolution. Whales, bats, deer, tapirs, pigs, camels, cattle, sloths, rodents, elephants, weasels, and many other mammals appeared with in a short period. Ten million years later, another burst of evolution produced seals, bears, dogs, cats, rabbits, rhinoceroses, and monkeys. These groups continued to change to produce the wide variety of mammals today.

TRIASSIC	JURASSIC	CRETACEOUS	PALEOCENE	EOCENE	OLIGOCENE	MIOCENE	PLIOCENE	PLEISTOCENE	HOLOCENE

PROTOTHERIANS — MONOTREMATA (platypus, echidnas)
MARSUPIALS (kangaroos, koalas, possums, bandicoots)
THERIANS — EDENTATA (anteaters, armadillos, sloths)
INSECTIVORA (hedgehogs, moles, shrews)
CHIROPTERA (bats)
PRIMATES (monkeys, lemurs, apes)
CREODONTA
CARNIVORA (cats, dogs, bears, weasels)
PINNIPEDIA (seals, walrus)
CETACEA (whales, dolphins)
PROBOSCIDEA (elephants)
SIRENIA (sea cows)
SOUTH AMERICAN UNGULATES
PERISSODACTYLS (horses, rhinos, tapirs)
ARTIODACTYLS (pigs, camels, deer, antelopes)
RODENTIA (mice, squirrels, cavies)
LAGOMORPHA (rabbits)

EUTHERIANS (PLACENTAL MAMMALS)

| MYA | | 213 | 144 | | 65 | 55 | 34 | 23 | 5 | 1,8 | 0,01 |

Recreating Dinosaurs for the Movies
A recreated dinosaur on film is the end result of years of work. Film directors use a combination of computer-generated animation and plastic models to bring the dinosaurs to life for the cameras. Paleontologists work with filmmakers to advise them about dinosaur appearance and behavior.

REBUILDING DINOSAURS

The expertise of paleontologists turns a pile of fossilized bones into a reconstructed dinosaur. As they study fossils and compare them with other animals, both living and extinct, scientists are able to discover what dinosaurs looked like and how they lived.

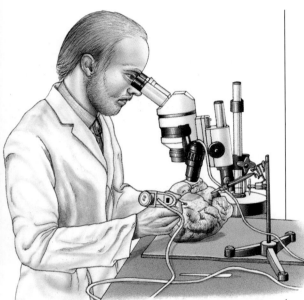

▲ A paleontologist peers through a high-powered microscope as he uses a vibrating needle to remove rock from around a delicate fossil bone.

Female

◀ *These drawings of two Protoceratops skulls are typical of those done as part of the study of a fossil. The more upright frill and bulging snout on the male may have been used as a signal.*

Male

STUDYING THE FOSSIL

Once the fossils are free of the rock, the scientist describes them. A scientific description is a lengthy process that involves very detailed drawings of the bones as well as highly technical language to identify the bones and show how they fit together. The scientist notes how the muscles and tendons attached to the bones. He or she also makes conclusions about the lifestyle of the dinosaur and how it may be related to others that have already been described.

The skull of a Gallimimus has a ▼ large eye, which suggests that it had good eyesight.

FREEING THE FOSSIL

When the fossil arrives at the laboratory, it is usually encased in a slab of rock that must be removed. Some rocks, such as limestone, can be removed by a soak in a weak acid solution. This eats away the rock, but leaves the mineral fossils unharmed. Other rocks need to be removed mechanically. Larger pieces are chipped off with a chisel, but more delicate tools are needed as the scientist gets closer to the fossil. A vibrating needle removes rock one grain at a time, and can be controlled so precisely that paleontologists use a microscope to guide them.

▶ *The arms of Deinocheirus end in long fingers with massive, curved claws. These would have been ideal to grip and tear prey.*

UNDERSTANDING MORE ABOUT DINOSAURS

Once the dinosaur skeleton has been put together and described, it is possible to learn more about the animal and its lifestyle. The teeth help in understanding what the dinosaur ate. Sharp pointed teeth mean the animal ate meat. Broad flat teeth usually mean it fed on plants. An animal with long, slender legs can usually run quickly, but one with short, squat legs can rarely move faster than a walk.

▶ *A fossil of a flowering plant. Some plants occur in rocks of a certain age only. Scientists who find such plants know how old the rocks are, even if there is no other way to date them.*

The glossy sheen on the skull and neck of this Iguanodon comes from a preservative used so the fossil will not crumble when exposed to air. ▶

FINDING OUT THE AGE OF THE FOSSIL

Scientists have not yet found a way to date a fossil itself. Instead, they date the rock in which it was found. Volcanic rocks are relatively easy to date. When molten rock runs out of a volcano, it has a specific amount of a radioactive chemical called Potassium 40. Over time, this breaks down and disappears at a set rate. If they measure how much Potassium 40 is left in the rock, scientists can determine how old it is. This works only with volcanic rocks, but fossils are usually found in sedimentary rocks such as sandstone or shale. Scientists look for a layer of volcanic rock near where fossils are found. This gives an approximate date.

THE MISSING LINKS

No matter how complete a fossil might be or how carefully it is described by scientists, the fact remains that dinosaurs are dead and there are some things that cannot be known for certain. For example, it is impossible to know what color the dinosaurs were. Based on modern animals, it has been suggested that dinosaurs had colorful skins used to help recognize each other or to signal. So far, no one can verify this theory. Sometimes, only part of a skeleton is found, so it is difficult to know what the rest of the animal looked like. The fossil of *Hylaeosaurus* was found with the back half missing. The fossil of *Polacanthus* was missing its front half. Some scientists think these are two halves of the same animal, but only if a complete skeleton is found can they know for sure.

Two different types of Iguanodon *fossil have been found.* Iguanodon mantelli *(right) is only about 20 feet (6 m) long.* Iguanodon bernissartenis *is 30 feet (9 m) long. It has been suggested that the two sizes represent the male and female of the same species. There is no way to prove this.*

▲ *This* Tyrannosaurus, *found in South Dakota, was named Sue after Sue Hendrickson, the paleontologist who discovered it.*

NEW LOCATIONS AND STUNNING FINDS

Scientists continue to search for dinosaur fossils and still make major discoveries. The deserts of Mongolia and northern China are among the most important new sites to be investigated. An American expedition found dinosaur fossils there in the 1920s, but revolution and unrest did not allow scientists to work there again for many years. In South Dakota in the 1990s, scientists discovered the most complete *Tyrannosaurus* skeleton ever found in North America. A total of 90 percent of the skeleton was unearthed.

◄ *The plastic bones are fitted together for display with the use of a crane.*

RECONSTRUCTING THE DINOSAUR

In the past, the dinosaur skeletons on display in museums were made of real fossils. The fossil bones were extremely heavy and had to be supported by metal rods and poles that spoiled the view. In recent years, scientists have begun to use plastic replicas of fossils. These are much lighter, so the skeletons can be placed in exciting poses that show dinosaurs as they attack or run swiftly. These new reconstructions give a much better idea of how dynamic and fascinating dinosaurs really were, compared with the old-fashioned skeletons that stood still. As a result, visitors to museums can find out much more about the dinosaurs and how they lived. The vast majority of actual dinosaur fossils remain in museum storerooms. Most fossils are bits of skeleton or even just a few teeth. They are vital to a proper scientific understanding of the dinosaurs. They are carefully cataloged and stored in numbered order. When a scientist wants to study a particular fossil, he or she knows where to find it.

A scientist makes a rubber mold ready to produce a plastic replica.
◄

Coelophysis was agile and fast-moving. It had hollow, bones that let it run swiftly.

In the movie *Jurassic Park*, a scientist recreates dinosaurs with genetic engineering. He takes dinosaur blood from the stomach of a mosquito preserved in amber and then uses the DNA to create entirely new dinosaurs. This is impossible for two reasons. First, the DNA extracted from insects in amber has deteriorated over the millions of years since they were alive, and only tiny fragments remain. Too much information is missing for scientists to put the pieces together to form a DNA code for a complete creature. Second, it is not possible to create an animal from DNA alone. Even if full dinosaur DNA codes were available, the DNA would need to be put into the eggs of a similar creature so that it could grow into a dinosaur. No animal alive today is similar enough to dinosaurs for this to happen.

THE FASTEST

Since there are no dinosaurs alive today, it is impossible to know how fast they ran. Scientists can estimate top speeds, however. They study the skeletons of dinosaurs and compare them with similar modern animals. It is thought that the fastest dinosaurs were the ornithomimosaurs, which had two very long legs with powerful muscles. These creatures might have been able to run about 31 miles (50 km) per hour for short distances.

THE BIGGEST, TALLEST, AND HEAVIEST

The largest dinosaurs were the sauropods. The longest was *Seismosaurus*, which grew up to 164 feet (50 m) long. The very long, thin tail made up much of this length. The shorter, but more solidly built, *Argentinosaurus* was the heaviest dinosaur. It weighed up to 100 tons. Both were relatively short compared with the *Brachiosaurus*, which held its long neck up to 39 feet (12 m) above ground to reach the very tops of trees.

◄ *A* Brachiosaurus *may have had an advantage over other plant-eaters. It could feed on plants out of the reach of its rivals.*

▲

An insect in amber, or fossilized tree sap. Amber preserves the animal perfectly, and some DNA can be extracted. The whole sequence needed to make an animal is not available, however.

A Giganotosaurus, *the largest of the hunting dinosaurs, was about 46 feet (14 m) long and weighed around 8 tons.*

▼

THE SMALLEST

Although people often think of dinosaurs as huge creatures, many were small and delicate. The plant-eating *Lesothosaurus* from southern Africa was just over 3^1/$_2$ feet (1 m) long and weighed around 22 pounds (10 kg). Most small dinosaurs, however, were meat-eaters that hunted mammals, lizards, and insects. The smallest were not as tall as a person's knee.

▲

The Compsognathus *was the smallest adult dinosaur. This tiny hunter was about 3^1/$_2$ feet (1 m) long and would have weighed about as much as a modern chicken.*

DINOSAUR RECORDS

The dinosaurs were among the most amazing creatures that ever lived. They were totally unlike any animal now alive. With their outsize body shapes, horns, and crests, they look bizarre today. The dinosaur group included some of the largest, heaviest, and fastest animals that have ever lived.

The head of a plesiosaur. These giant sea reptiles were not dinosaurs. They were from a different group of extinct reptiles. ▼

DINOSAUR MYTHS

Many myths have developed about dinosaurs over the years. One common error is to think that all reptiles from the Mesozoic Era were dinosaurs. Only the reptiles that lived on land were dinosaurs. Although dinosaurs may have entered water to feed or drink, they were not good swimmers. Flying pterosaurs were not dinosaurs, either. Dinosaurs could not fly. Another myth is that dinosaurs became extinct because they were stupid. They may have had brains that were smaller than those of modern mammals, but their brains were larger and more complex than those of other reptiles.

THE SMARTEST AND THE DUMBEST

Scientists have found that the intelligence of an animal is related to the ratio between the size of its brain and the size of its body. This ratio is called the encephalization quotient. Based on this figure, the most intelligent dinosaur was the *Troodon*, a 10-foot-long (3 m) hunter from the end of the Cretaceous. It was about as intelligent as a modern crow or rook. The least intelligent was the *Stegosaurus*, which had a brain as big as a walnut in a body weighing about 2 tons.

THE OLDEST KNOWN

The two-legged *Herrerasaurus* (above) was long considered the earliest dinosaur. It lived in the middle of the Triassic, about 227 mya. However, prosauropod remains recently found in Madagascar date to 230 mya. In 2001, even older fossils were found in southern Brazil. They came from a carnivorous dinosaur 6 1/2 feet (2 m) long that lived about 240 mya.

Some scientists believe that if the dinosaurs had not become extinct, Troodon may have evolved to become as intelligent as modern humans. They have named this imaginary creature "dinosaurid." ◄

◄ *Iguanodon was one of the most successful dinosaurs of its time. The dinosaurs were not a failure—they ruled the world for 150 million years. So far, modern humans (Homo sapiens) have only existed for about 120,000 years.*

THE MOST DANGEROUS

The most dangerous dinosaurs were those from a group known as dromaeosaurids. These were fast runners that lived in the Cretaceous Period, from about 120 to 65 mya. They had large, curved claws on their hind legs, which they held above the ground when they walked so they stayed razor sharp, but swung forward when they attacked prey. The front legs also had curved talons used to hold prey while the hind leg kicked forward—a deadly combination.

► *Like all birds, this swallow is a descendant of dinosaurs. Because birds evolved from dinosaurs, some argue that dinosaurs are not really extinct.*

▲ *Deinonychus is the best known of the dromaeosaurids. It was equipped with a "terrible claw."*

INDEX